THE STONE AGE BABY in a TECHNO SOCIETY

Nancy Williams, Margie Deutsch Lash MSEd, Gretchen Andrews, with Shawn Crane

ISBN: 146095985X
ISBN 13: 9781460959855

ACKNOWLEDGEMENTS:

The authors gratefully acknowledge and thank La Leche League International for teaching us how to mother and share with those who came after us. The idea of this book was born around the meeting table of the Professional Liaison Department of La Leche League of Southern California/Nevada, among friends who have supported and challenged and taught each other for many years.

We are further thankful to Rachele Burke and Nils Bergman for the generous sharing of ideas and information.

Kathy Nesper, Kathleen Whitfield, and Heather Lang graciously gave of their time and talent in editing; we thank them.

Timothy Pack (packgraphics.com) provided the drawing of the Stoneage mother and baby. We deeply appreciate the talent he shared.

Our deepest love and thanks to our families; supportive husbands and children and grandchildren for whom we deeply long for a loving world.

This book is lovingly dedicated to the thousands of mother-baby pairs that the four of us have had the privilege of caring for and helping for the last 35 plus years.

Together the authors have over 100 years of experience working with mothers, babies and children in the fields of childbirth, lactation, and education. While coming from very different backgrounds and worldviews, they are uniquely suited to discussing these issues of utmost importance to babies, children, parents, and most important society at-large. Enlightenment and empowerment can only exist in a world where people are aware of the problems that affect their daily lives.

Nancy Williams, MA, MFT, IBCLC, CCE

Prior to becoming a mother, Nancy served families as a youth pastor's wife, transitioning to working with mothers and babies in 1975, becoming a certified childbirth educator shortly after. She has been a La Leche League Leader for over 30 years, and an International Board Certified Lactation Consultant since 1986. As her children became more independent, she returned to school for her MA in psychology and became a licensed Marriage and Family Therapist in 1996. She maintains a small private practice and has many years of experience supporting adolescent mothers through pregnancy care centers. She is an adjunct faculty member of Brandman (formerly Chapman) University College, Santa Maria Campus, teaching in the psychology department with a concentration in Human Development. She is intensely interested in bridging information between the fields of perinatal medicine and education with psychology, most especially Attachment Theory and other current information regarding Infant Development.

Nancy is the author of a chapter in a book, two editions of a booklet for Lactation Consultants, as well as articles in Journal of Human Lactation, New Beginnings and other periodicals. She is the recipient of a community award, Woman of Excellence: Women helping Women and was Adjunct Faculty of the Year for Chapman University College Santa Maria Campus in 2008.

Margie Deutsch Lash, MSEd, IBCLC, E-RYT

Since 1975, Margie has been working with children and families in a variety of roles. Her work has included being an elementary school teacher, specializing in early childhood education, a school director, a La Leche League Leader, an International Board Certified Lactation Consultant, a parenting consultant, and a yoga teacher specializing in yoga therapy. Her education at the University of Southern California, which includes both bachelor and master degrees in education, afforded her the opportunity to learn from educators (most notably Dr. Margaret Smart) who imparted their wisdom about child development and the manner in which children learn, in such an effective manner, that Margie has felt it her obligation to assist families to learn about their children. She sees her work as assisting society to provide the kind of support that children require to grow into healthy, well-adjusted human beings, who will be able to guide the planet into the next century. She was a contributing author and a regular columnist for Paths of Learning, a learning journal that was in print until 2005. Margie is a popular speaker at conferences attended by lactation professionals and parents.

Gretchen Andrews, IBCLC, BA, RLC

With the birth of her first of three children in 1984 Gretchen's career focus moved from engineering to the special needs of mothers and babies. She became a La Leche League Leader in 1986 and began her studies to become a lactation consultant following the birth of her youngest child. Upon earning her International Board Certified Lactation Consultant status in 1991 she began a private practice and has extensive experience working in hospitals, public health centers and out-patient facilities. She co-founded the first breastfeeding clinic in the Inland Empire of Los Angeles County, which provided a model for several other clinics in the Los Angeles area. Gretchen served as adjunct faculty at the Lactation Institute in Encino, CA and currently serves as President of Inland Empire breastfeeding coalition. In addition she participates on the Leadership Team of the California Breastfeeding Coalition and participates in many activities on the national level.

Shawn Crane, BA

Shawn Crane has been supporting and educating mothers and children since 1991. As a La Leche Leader she has provided information for mothers on breastfeeding, parenting, and nurturing their babies. Her work as an Assistant Area Professional Liaison with La Leche League allowed her to provide a bridge between mothers and the medical and legal profession in breastfeeding and parenting. She has studied lactation, maternal issues and infant development at the Lactation Institute in California. As the director of Youth Leadership Project, and Crane Academy of Excellence two small private schools in California she has worked closely with families and has seen the positive impact that strong attachment and proper early childrearing practices has on the formation of adolescence, teens, and young adults. She is currently pursuing her Masters degree in Education.

PREFACE

BY NANCY WILLIAMS

"The newborn has only three demands. They are warmth in the arms of its mother, food from her breasts, and security in the knowledge of her presence. Breastfeeding satisfies all three."

— Grantly Dick-Read

It has not become cliché to mention how fast our world is changing. With the advent of exponentially advancing knowledge, technology and consequent abilities, time travelers arriving from just twenty-five years ago might not even recognize our world. By and large, these developments have given us opportunity for better things: longer lives, better economic status, good health and excellent care when we are ill or injured, to name a few benefits.

At the same time, we are witnessing increasing relational/psychological/sociological problems. Just fifty years ago high school principals lamented the trouble they were having with boys who swore and chewed gum in class. I don't know any school administrator who wouldn't give anything to have that be his or her most pressing issues today. For the first time ever, attention is being given to serious mental health problems in young children, including bipolar disorder in kindergartners and depression in infants. Permanent family constellations are becoming less common with divorce rates holding fairly steady at around 50%. The current generation of young adults is marrying later—or not at all—often citing their own fear of failure, having witnessed so many broken marriages around them. The list goes on of dramatic societal changes experienced in American culture in just the most recent generations.

Why? What has changed?

Despite our ever-evolving culture with its attendant perks as well as losses, the one thing that hasn't changed is the basic needs of human beings. We are hardwired with certain needs, expectations and requirements for healthy functioning. Besides oxygen and food, perhaps the most constant need of human beings is to be in relationship. We crave attachment to another. From our earliest moments of extra-uterine life human babies can be observed engaging in behaviors that seek out loving responses from the adult(s) who should be primed to respond warmly and affectionately. The greatest pain in our lives is not caused by physical trauma but by rejection, abandonment, or loneliness.

This book is an attempt to understand how we may be failing to meet the needs of the most vulnerable of our population—our babies and children. Since the Stone Age, the needs of babies have remained the same: Babies need food and oxygen, warmth and protection, and generous amount of constant love and affection. Current practices beginning even before birth often hinder the baby's access to or the mother's delivery of these desperately needed yet simple things.

The wonders of technology are here to stay; babies are biologically mandated with certain needs and expectations. Perhaps as our society continues to evolve, we would do well to find ways to wed the best of technology with optimal support of biology, safeguarding our most vulnerable members in order to ensure a healthy future for all.

Note from authors:

Of course we know that babies delightfully come in both sexes. For sake of clarity we will refer to baby as "he" since mother is invariably "she".

WHO IS THE STONE AGE BABY?

BY GRETCHEN ANDREWS

Have babies' needs changed significantly since our earliest ancestors arrived on Earth? The world they arrive into has certainly changed and is such a contrast from what they expect. The first human babies did not arrive in sanitized, antiseptic, austere hospitals. In fact, only in the past century has being born in a hospital become our cultural norm. Prior to the availability of white, starched uniforms and nearly sterile conditions, babies were generally brought into the world in the same bed in which they were conceived.

Our earliest ancestors were born into considerably less hospitable environs than today's world of supermarkets and shopping malls. When a soon-to-be-mother was coming to term in her pregnancy, the "nesting urge" would compel her to create a safe, sheltered place where she could do the work of her labor, deliver her baby and recover for a period of time before having to return to eking out an existence. Likely, she lived within a group of other people who could provide her with food and maintain shelter for her during her physical recovery. The weight she added during her pregnancy would help sustain her if food was scarce following her delivery. The placenta, which nourished her unborn baby, could also provide maternal nourishment when the baby was finished using it.

But what about her new baby? As the fetus grew uncomfortably large housed in the ever increasing snugness of his mother's body, there came a time when the rhythms changed. He was pressed, squeezed, and ultimately catapulted from her body after a long or short series of contractions and pushes. Suddenly, the temperature was different: it may have been cold; it may have been much hotter, but it sure wasn't what it used to be anymore. As the baby entered into life outside the womb and took his first breath, everything changed. His own circulatory system was independent now and must function on its own. Soon, the life-sustaining organ that had provided all of his nutrition since his conception ceased to pulse. His food supply was gone. As his mother held his naked body next to her own, he began to sense an inner urge to search for a new source of nutrition. From his resting place on his mother's abdomen, he could smell the familiar scent of the fluid being emitted from the Montgomery glands around the areola of his mother's breast. He was compelled to crawl his way to his mother's chest where he would enjoy the warmth and comfort that it offered. The amniotic fluid, although dry, still covered his own body, and he sucked his hands as he had done in utero. The scent from the region near the nipple beckoned him, and he sought to find this new yet familiar place. As he crawled closer, the feel of the nipple on his check told him he was nearly there. After some more mouthing on his hands, he could finally see his mother's face clearly, and he wormed his way over to the center of her breast, opened wide and took his mother's nipple deep into his mouth and began to suckle.

This suckling began a sequence of events inside his mother's body as well. In response to his tugging at her breast, hormones were released to begin the domino effect on her body. The colostrum her body had been preparing for this new life began to flow into him with his gentle suckling, and oxytocin was released, which had a cramping affect on her uterus that helped expel the placenta baby had abandoned. This cramping also helped reduce the amount of maternal bleeding so mother would be strong enough to nutritionally support the two of them. As the suckling continued, hormones also initiated feelings of tenderness for her new baby. As she stroked her child and he responded in kind, the beginning of the attachment that would secure his survival began. It is no coincidence that baby mammals are born interminably cute. The roundness in their features and their softness all contribute to creating bonds that will make those capable of protecting them wish to do so. The affection that develops in the give and take during and between feedings cements an indelible bond that ensures the baby's very survival.

Was the place his mother chose to bring him into the world full of glaring lights and harsh loud noises? Highly unlikely. Like most mammals readying themselves for birth, she would have sought out somewhere protected, maybe enclosed, and surely away from most others. As her baby was born into the world of light, it would at least begin with dim illumination. His limited ability to see let him clearly focus on only the most necessary parts of his new life—his mother's face, her breasts, and her fingers and hands as she touched his body. He could respond joyfully during their mutual gazes and touching. As long as he was in her arms, all was right with his world. And so it was for eons. Babies remained with their mothers following their birth to be nurtured and grow until the urges within them prompted locomotion away from mother gradually as their abilities increased.

Of course, in many instances, mothers or babies did not survive birth. If the mother was lost and no other mother offered herself, the baby would soon join his mother in the hereafter. His mother, or a functional mother substitute, was essential to the baby's survival.

As you can see, human beings haven't always arrived on the planet via hospitals with a medical staff in attendance. Long before doctors, nurses, or midwives, human babies were born like other mammals and survived well enough to have populated the entire planet. How on Earth did these early humans survive without medical intervention and assistance? Perhaps some of the clues to early human survival are visible by observing other mammalian species.

When other mammals, such as puppies, kittens, or bunnies, are born, we expect the babies to instinctively know how to squirm their way to their mother's teat and begin to suckle. We wouldn't dream of interrupting this process or of separating these babies from their mothers, because babies who do not make the journey to their mother's teat successfully are not likely to survive. Access to a mother is necessary for survival for baby mammals of all species.

There are four categories of mammals determined by feeding methodology. Cache animals, such as baby bunnies, are left alone for extended periods while their mother forages for food. They are fed about twice a day, and their mother's milk is high in fat to sustain such extended separation. Nesting animals, such as dogs and cats, are periodic feeders. Their mother's milk is not as high in fat content because it does not need to sustain the nestlings as long between feedings. Follow animals, such as cows and horses, have the ability to keep up with their mothers within hours after birth and thus can feed frequently. The fat content of their mother's milk is lower still, since babies do not have to wait for extended periods between feedings. Carry mammals, such as primates, have nearly constant contact with their mother and can feed almost continuously. Their mother's milk is very low in fat, because feedings are intended to be quite frequent. Then too, human milk is also a dynamic food whose composition varies immensely during the course of lactation, from one feeding to another, from day to day, and across mother and baby pairs.

Protective Factors of Breastmilk

The human newborn gut is extremely immature at birth. Mother's breastmilk is perfectly adapted to help provide immunological protection. Of the over 350 identified components in human milk, many play a key role in the baby's immune function rather than just a nutrition function. 60–70 percent of breastmilk protein is composed of whey, which is important for this protection. Immunoglobulins protect baby from infection; immunostimulants protect baby from allergies, and immunosupressives dampen inflammation in the baby's system.

Only 8 percent of human milk is casein (one of the proteins found in mammalian milks), while the ratio of whey to casein in cow's milk, the substance used most often in artificial infant milk (AIM), that is, formula, is nearly the reverse—formula is composed of 90 percent casein and 8 percent whey. Then too, AIM is a static food. It is not alive. It does not respond to changes in a baby's needs as human milk does. Also, cow's milk, on which most commercial formulas are based, is designed for a calf—a mature-born infant with four stomachs, a follow animal—not for an immature human with a single stomach. As a result, formulas are much more difficult to digest than breastmilk for human infants.

Even though over 350 components in human have been identified, countless other trace components remain unidentified. Human milk is unique in its ability to nourish human babies while protecting them from diseases and maximizing their growth potential. The protection from diseases such as diarrhea, respiratory tract infections, neonatal sepsis (blood infections), ear infections, and pneumonia is not available via any man-made source. Breastmilk substitutes can provide sufficient calories and much of the nutrition required by babies, but no substitute can protect against disease. Even our arsenal of antibiotics and other medications can only work on disease after it has begun, and they don't prevent the suffering of those afflicted with illnesses. Although we have made great strides in protecting our babies and children through the use of vaccines, even those work much more effectively in babies that are breastfed where baby's exposure via mother's immune system has laid a path of protection.

Place and Behavior

A discovery in the mid-1800s not only profoundly affected childbirth and childcare practices but also shaped a new notion of normalcy for birth and the sequel of events surrounding birth and infancy: germ theory was developed and antiseptic processes were introduced. On the positive side, theses resulted in a huge reduction in maternal morbidity (sickness) and mortality (death). However, like many good things, germ theory went a bit too far, and by the end of the nineteenth century infection thought to be contracted from mothers was blamed for deaths in preterm infants. One result of this misconception was the invention of the incubator (initially referred to as the "child hatchery"). It was constructed of glass so that mothers of preterm infants could see their babies and be *part of the team* caring for *their* babies. This idea was unfortunately exploited by Martin Cooney; he took infants who had been born premature and were not expected to live, raised them in incubators, and exhibited them at the World's Fair in 1896.

While Cooney was responsible for helping save the lives of many babies who might have died, he also eliminated mothers from the care of these fragile infants. They were returned to their mothers after they reached five pounds, but their mothers were not permitted to visit them prior to that. This evolved into a routine practice of keeping all babies in the protective custody of obstetric nurses rather than leaving them to be cared for by their own mothers. The notion that mother was a source of infection for newborns became popular, and with the advent of infant formula, mothers became unnecessary in this healthcare model.

Except the notion wasn't true. Like all young mammals, human infants are programmed to operate within a particular habitat—with their mother. Newborn babies have consistently demonstrated extraordinary capabilities to function in their natural habitat of their mothers' arms. Newborn babies will seek nourishment, comfort, and warmth by crawling to their mother's breast and suckling. In all mammals, it is the baby who initiates this process. Imagine what must happen when a tactilely sensitive baby is wrapped up like a burrito and presented to his mother with no way to use his body to connect with hers! When placing babies in either incubators or isolettes became acceptable and commonplace, a huge interruption of the connection between mother and baby began.

The sequence of behaviors by babies following birth are determined by the neonate stimulating the mother—not the other way around (Rosenblatt, 1994). The newborn is responsible for initiating breastfeeding (Kjellmar & Winberg, 1994). Further, as has been documented many times over but was first filmed by Swedish researchers Righard and Adele in 1991, when a baby is placed on his mother's chest, skin to skin, shortly following birth, the baby will begin a series of behaviors culminating with suckling at the breast. While on his mother's bare chest, he will begin to bring his hand to his mouth, move his tongue and mouth, focus his eyes on and crawl toward the nipple, as he gazes at his mother's face from time to time until he latches on to her breast with a wide open mouth and begins to suckle.

If baby is not with mother, if instead he is separated for whatever reason, this process cannot occur. Babies who are placed in isolettes or on warming tables are removed from the only place they know how to begin life—mother. Despite countless arguments about why babies need to be places other than on their mothers, short of the need for full resuscitation, almost any postnatal procedure is better off being done while baby is in skin-to-skin contact with mother.

When babies are separated from their mothers—their niche, their habitat—the universal response is despair. "Where is my mother?" If separation is prolonged, babies begin to shut down in a way that resembles sleep but is actually a conservation of resources to survive. Heart, respiration, and blood pressure levels are higher in isolated infants than in a baby sleeping peacefully in its normal habitat, with mother.

We would never consider removing the young of any other mammal without the expectation of dire consequences, yet we have become so accustomed to this routine separation of human babies in the past century or so that it has become the new normal in the Western world.

Walking into the newborn nursery of a typical American hospital, one is generally greeted by babies crying for their mothers. This depletes both their energy and oxygen reserves, increases white blood cell counts, and bathes babies' brains in toxic hormones, like cortisol, that are extremely harmful to developing brains. With the development of trust (Erickson, 1963) being a primary objective in the first year of life, the process is hardly helped by the way we have kept mothers and babies separated in our modern hospital systems.

Nils Bergman's (a Public Health physician and expert on skin-to-skin contact) research as well as that of other primate researchers, has determined that in the immediate post partum period, the normal biological habitat for human newborns is skin-to-skin contact (2006). The infant seeks to adhere to as much skin surface on the mother's body as possible (Harlow, 1958). The tactile stimulation resulting from skin-to-skin contact promotes growth in the brain's amygdala, part of the limbic or lower brain area related to emotions, during the first eight weeks of life. This pathway development requires eye-to-eye contact, a natural by-product of skin-to-skin and breastfeeding, and is the basis of healthy right brain development. The right brain is responsible for brain-to-brain interaction, face-to-face communication, and eye-to-eye orientations, as well as voice, hand, and movement control and the awareness of interpersonal emotions.

According to guidelines created by the International Primate Society (IPS) in 1993, young primates should not be separated from their mothers at an early age (that is, less than 6 months old). IPS guidelines further stipulate that mother/baby pairs should remain in physical contact for 12 to 18 months in monkeys such as macaques, baboons, and capuchins, and infants should not be weaned before 6 months. Based on research beginning with Harry Harlow's primate studies in the 1950s, we know that rearing infants in isolation (apart from their mothers) induces pervasive behavioral problems. They develop abnormal behavior patterns such as bizarre postures, self-clasping, or self-aggression. Rhesus monkeys removed from their social groups exhibited symptoms of depression, which can be measured by adrenal cortisol response as well as long-term depression of the immune system.

In even in the small mammal *Octodon degus*, a South American rodent, a minimal separation of only ten minutes two times a day from days eight to ten altered brain functions, induced receptor changes, and contributed to the pathophysiology of a variety of clinical disorders.

Babies cared for with skin-to-skin contact (SSC) have physical protection provided by mother, immune protection from mother's milk, and neurological protection from stress, which leads to better immunity later in life (Bergman, 2006).

Then too, there is greater sleep synchrony when mother and baby are together. Mothers also have fewer problems such as engorgement and infections when mother and baby are together.

Habitat Determines Behavior

Skin to skin contact does not have any adverse affects. Human milk is the post-birth continuation of the habitat of the immature human being. Only marsupials are born less completely developed than human infants, and nature has provided a pouch for them to stay in to be protected, fed, and cared for until they are sufficiently developed to care for themselves. Although human babies need no pouch, their mothers' milk is critical for nutrition, warmth, oxygenation and protection.

When baby is placed skin to skin on mother, generally within 5 minutes the baby's heart rate stabilizes, and respirations become regular.

Temperature control in an incubator occurs within a "stable" range that is considerably more erratic than what occurs when baby and mother are kept together. In contrast, when baby is on his mother, the thermal synchrony is at a higher range than in an incubator. Newly delivered mother's have chest core temperature 1 degree Celsius higher than other women to help maintain their babies' thermal requirements.

Our reproductive behavior has changed over the past three generations, and that timeline is way too short for babies to adapt; it violates their innate agenda. We need to protect the integrity of the mother baby dyad.

Sensory stimulation between women and men is built from countless exchanges of subtle clues, clues that begin at birth. Maternal regulators govern all elements of the baby's physiology: heart rate, hormones, appetite, and activity.

Early brain development is interactive, rapid, and dramatic. During critical periods, specific stimulations are required at specific times. Quality sensory stimulation makes the brain able to think and regulate negative experiences (the absence of good as well as the presence of bad), and this infant stimulation has long-lasting effects.

Hofer states "Mother is baby's environment" (1994).Physical functions, such as grooming and nursing, as well as the stimuli of touch, balance, smell, hearing, and vision all have specific effects on the infant. McCain (1999) states that multiple sensory inputs via several pathways simultaneously align [the] wiring of the brain's pathways.

Within the first three years of life, the limbic system (which regulates attachment, regulation, emotion, control) and the midbrain (which is in charge of arousal, appetite, and sleep) become fixed. Both of these serve as platforms for subsequent development of higher cognitive function. The limbic system further houses neurobehavior programs through the hypothalamus (autonomic nervous system), the hypophysis (endocrine system and hormones), and cerebellar connections in the somatic system.

The difference between humans and other animals is the development of the cerebral cortex. The hindbrain still remains vital, controlling its three essential programs of defense, nutrition and reproduction.

TABLE 1

Essential human functions and their associated systems

	Defense	**Nutrition**	**Reproduction**
Receptors	Hormones	Nerves	Muscles
Regulatory system	Endocrine	Autonomic nervous	Somatic*

*** Somatic is a developmental trauma referring to various kinds of psychological damage that occur during child development when a child has insufficient attention from the primary caregivers or an insufficiently nurturing relationship with the parent.**

The current generally accepted paradigm of infant brain development holds that

- Development is genetically determined.
- The brain develops in linear time.
- Brain activity increases with age.
- The mother is a universally good context.
- Deficits are correctable later.

New research indicates these premises are false.

The new paradigm suggests that experience and critical periods are most receptive within the first three years. This early development promotes the hardwiring of the brain, and the limbic brain is fixed by completion of the third year. The mammalian brain is designed to be sculpted into its final configuration by the effects of early experience, although the brain's cortex retains some plasticity throughout life.

At birth, the human baby has more brain synapses than at any other stage of life. According to Rima Shore, a critical period, a window of opportunity, exists in early life when a child's brain is exquisitely primed to receive sensory input to develop more advanced neural systems (1997). When babies receive the sensory input that is a byproduct of skin-to-skin contact, they are in a prime environment to create optimal growth for this neural system. Tactile input and kinetic sensations are critical for brain maturation.

Recall Harlow's assertion; "The infant seeks to adhere to as much skin surface on the mother's body as possible" (1958). All mammals have a set sequence of behaviors at birth with a single purpose—to breastfeed. Although newborns may appear helpless, they display purposeful motor activity which brings baby to the breast without maternal assistance (Michelson et al, 1996).

Fast-forward to modern times. Along with hospitals came rules—arbitrary rules, not the rules of nature. Mothers were considered dirty. Babies were viewed as fragile and highly susceptible to falling sick. Therefore, babies should be kept in as sterile an environment as possible, in a clean nursery attended by scrubbed and antiseptic nurses in their starched uniforms. And because babies were kept away from their mothers, rules were needed for bringing babies (wrapped in hospital blankets like tiny burritos) to their mothers. With many babies and few nurses to care for them, babies could be brought to their mothers only at intervals scheduled conveniently (for the nurses)—usually every four hours. And because mothers were "dirty," their breasts needed to be cleaned thoroughly. Never mind that Mother Nature had already taken care of this via the Montgomery glands around the areolar complex that clean and lubricate the breast automatically; bring on the Betadine, and scrub those nasty dirty nipples. Is it any wonder that limiting feedings to such nonphysiologic times produced a plethora of women who couldn't make sufficient milk for their babies?

In the meantime, baby has lost the only thing he truly needs to survive—his mother. He may be brought to her at regularly scheduled intervals, which may or may not coincide with his internal program for waking and feeding. If babies and mothers sustain care like this for several days to a week, is it any wonder American women ceased to be able to breastfeed, and infants required bottles filled initially with physician-prescribed concoctions of PET Milk and Karo Syrup and ultimately with commercially produced AIMs taken from unsuspecting cows depriving their calves of their mother's milk?

Back to our Stone Age baby—as limited as human newborns were and are, they still possess sufficient skills to participate in their own survival. The innate crawling reflex that allows a baby to seek out, locate, and attach to the breast addressed a paramount. The grasping reflex of a newborn may well have assisted in helping him cling to mother's hair, skin, or clothing to maintain physical closeness with the one on whom he depended for all his needs. Babies are quite capable of communicating long before they can use verbal or sign language express their needs. Different tones in a baby's cry or babbling are easily recognized by an observant mother.

The attachment of mother and child was a given in early human societies. It was necessary for physical survival. For eons, keeping mothers and their babies together was the norm in human social interactions. As we moved as a species into stratified classes, these long-standing practices were disrupted. Women of the elite upper classes during the Victorian era became considered too delicate for breastfeeding. The use of wet nurses became an elective and popular practice, which led to an excessive number of births for these women for whom the child-spacing advantages afforded by breastfeeding were denied. Then too, the use of a wet nurse was sometimes relegated as an activity outside the palace gates. As an interesting aside, in many cases, babies were given over to a wet nurse in the country to suckle and then returned when the child was weaned. There is suspicion that perhaps the switching of children belonging to the wet nurse occurred. Because of the high level of inbreeding between European royal families the introduction of new DNA to the gene pool may have been quite helpful.

As further evidence of the value of the mother-baby dyad, when foundling homes were first begun in the eighteenth century the death rate was extremely high—nearly 90 percent of infants failed to survive. Even when appropriate food (donated human milk) and hygiene were furnished to these babies, the lack of human touch and interaction meant the vast majority failed to thrive. Human and other primate babies need adequate amounts of human touch—continuous human contact—to survive.

As various parenting methods come in vogue, babies become the unwitting pawns in a game whose rules can't be bent too much without dire consequences. Babies who are denied the comfort of their mothers' arms and the milk from their breasts need to finding that comfort and nurturance elsewhere. A baby clinging to a soft toy and sucking desperately on a pacifier has become the modern vision of normalcy in Western culture. The needs of babies have not changed. The response to them accepted by society has. Social expectations have evolved at exponential rates, but babies are still Stone Age people at heart.

"Society reaps what it sows in the way that infants and children are treated. Efforts to reduce exposure to stress and abuse in early life may have far-reaching impacts on medical and psychiatric health and may reduce aggression, suspicion and untoward stress in future generations."

-- Martin H. Teicher

INTRODUCTION

BY NANCY WILLIAMS

The biggest disease today is not leprosy or cancer. It's the feeling of being uncared for, unwanted—of being deserted and alone.

--Mother Teresa

Once upon a time, often during the still of the night, babies were born in the quiet of the home they would live and grow in. As Mother pushed a baby into the world, he would be bundled onto her chest, placed near her life-sustaining breasts, not for just the next few minutes, but to spend much of early extrauterine life both waking and sleeping near to her in order to access the nurturing and sweet milk of her breasts. Unknowingly, as the mother cared for his physical needs she was also creating a solid foundation for mental, social, and spiritual health.

For his first nine months, as he gestated, the baby and mother were one, united in body and soul. On the continuum of their relationship, the two entered a new stage at birth. Nursing brought a new unity of their bodies, driving this most important human relationship that he will ever know.

Most babies grow and develop in the context of a fiercely loving, protective "she-bear" of a mother. In her arms, he "learned" what it was to love, how to engage with others, when to be fearful or cautious and, as he grew, how to self-comfort and to begin to cognitively assess his world. His brain developed a rich synaptic network, as his mother stimulated all areas simply by including him in her experiences and attending to his needs. The love in her eyes, her smile, and her constant touch all served to tell him that he was wonderful, thus developing a secure self-image, preventing narcissistic desperation to seek his value elsewhere.

Life offers the opportunity for many joyful experiences in intimacy, yet he will know only a few that are as intense as this one. Healthy marriage contains the experience of intimacy on all levels, creating an emotional safe harbor for a lifetime of events. The mother-baby relationship is the only other affiliation in life that offers that level of intimacy: physical oneness, spiritual connection, psychological synchrony, relational satisfaction. Breastfeeding is the only experience besides sex and gestation where one's body is actually joined to another.

Fast-Forward to the Later 21st Century

A baby may or may not gestate for nine months in his mother's womb, now commonly evicted at the pleasure of someone's work or family schedule. He is likely separated from her at the moment of birth, spending many hours away to satisfy hospital requirements. When Baby is brought in, the two are separated by layers of blankets. Mother may not be comfortable enough to hold him in a way that facilitates cuddling because her episiotomy or cesarean incision is too painful. She may even be reeling from the frank trauma of a birth experience gone awry. Her maternal brain, designed with perfect hormonal "soup," an exquisite combination of necessary and helpful chemicals to facilitate mothering, may be compromised by a dysfunctional birth that failed to trigger the proper chemicals and then further compromised by the presence of one or more drugs. Rather than lovingly studying every facet of her new baby's beautiful body, she may be texting and sending pictures to her Facebook page. If he was born by cesarean, her brain may not respond normally to his cry. Finally she is uncomfortable nursing her baby in the ever-present company of a parade of visitors, whose presence interferes with the establishment of bonding and then breastfeeding.

When they go home, they probably return to a context filled with demands for her to do anything and everything except settle in to a "babymoon," similar to a honeymoon with the focus on each other and on developing intimacy and enjoying deepening knowledge of the other. Instead, her books have told her to create structure and to set the schedule for feeding and sleeping. She has heard precious little about adjusting to the "new normal", with life changed forever. Cultural expectations sustained by media depictions of parenthood have instead hinted to her that in short order everything ought to be back to the way it was before Baby—especially if she "does it right". She perceives breastfeeding as just that: "feeding" by breast. Little mention is made of nursing as the catalyst for the developing love between them.

Shortly after that, she may return to work, spending most of the baby's waking hours away. His first smiles, reaches, steps, and relational competence will likely be observed by the daycare provider, rather than shared with his mother.

⌘ ⌘ ⌘

When my nephew, now a medical student, was only two years old, he used to "read" his favorite book to anyone who would sit with him. It was the story of a baby bird who had fallen out of his nest and gone searching for his mother. Baby Bird asked everybody from a dog to a bulldozer if they were his mother, finally finding her at the end of a long, lonely quest. Sad as his pursuit was, birds can do quite well on their own once out of the nest. Beyond the fledgling stage, they have no need of their mother.

⌘ ⌘ ⌘

Humans, on the other hand, are mammals, and all mammals have a critical need for their mothers for varying amounts of time. Additionally, humans are "carrying mammals," closer to other species whose babies also grow and develop on their backs, chests, and in their arms. The very survival of a mammal is dependent on access to Mother. Unique among mammals, though, humans have complex relational needs and abilities, are deeply spiritual, and rely on lifelong attachments in families, communities, and other relational contexts. Their souls require more looking after!

This book is being written to sound an alarm. Western practices, particularly in the United States, are resulting in a new experience for babies. Rather than spending the first years in the arms of the person who loves them the most, they have a limbic (i.e. emotional) experience that is similar to our baby bird. Therapists often spend much of their time assisting people with the healing of wounds inflicted by the physical and emotional absence of Mother in early life.

This is to our detriment.

A Word About Guilt

Consistently as this information is presented in workshops and conferences around the United States, loud objections are raised. "Why do you want to make mothers feel guilty?" "Safe births are more important than satisfying births." "Mothers have to work, so this is impractical." One health care professional said that we need to tell families the truth so that they can make the best possible decision. Twenty minutes later when data was presented that contradicted the choices made by her own adult children (affecting her grandchildren), she remarked, "I don't want to hear that. Don't say it."

Let's talk about guilt. The dictionary defines guilt as *"an awareness of having done wrong or committed a crime, accompanied by feelings of shame and regret."* Generally, we feel guilty after doing something we know to be wrong, such as lying to a friend. Guilt has a positive, healthy function. It helps us not to repeat our transgression, so we apologize to our friend and tell her the truth, vowing honesty in the future. Guilt becomes less functional when it just sits in our psyche making us miserable, rather than serving its purpose. I've often felt heavy sadness remembering how I left my first baby to cry alone as a regular occurrence, remembering her beautiful face contorted in fear and anger. Is this guilt?

Perhaps regarding our parenting the guilt that we think we feel may be in fact, regret. The Dictionary defines regret thus, *"to feel sadness about something, or feel a sense of loss and longing for somebody or something that is no longer there."* [1] Regret is often a strong, negative twin sister of guilt but sometimes mistaken for it. The sadness of regret often quickly gives way to anger, looking for someone to blame. I've come to recognize that my sadness is regret, much more than it is guilt. Had I known that what I was doing was hurtful, and done it anyway, guilt may have been the primary emotion. But I didn't know until later that what I was doing was harming my baby. I didn't understand.

But I Didn't Know

The vast majority of parents love their children more than their own lives. Parents do the best they can with the information and resources available to them. We are prepared—for good or otherwise—for our parenting roles from the time we are children, influenced by our own parents, the media, families in our neighborhoods, religious beliefs, and our education. Often there are serious lapses in our preparation to be parents.

Perhaps much of our mother-angst is born out of conflict between what our hearts and instincts tell us is right and what our heads have been conditioned to believe might be best. Personally, I experienced a great deal of inner conflict and turmoil as I parented and then learned about child development, often when it was too late to implement it with my children, particularly the oldest. I wish I had known then what I know now. My heart told me to pick up my baby and love on her but my mind, influenced by people and books, told me not to. So I missed out and she was hurt.

Healing my own attachment wounds has been a long process. Talking with my daughter, wise friends and a couple of wonderful

1 **Encarta Dictionary: English (North American).**

therapists has been helpful. Reading and understanding has further contributed to resolution of the pain.

How much better for us to avoid making decisions that will invite the company of these twins of painful guilt and regret into our life. We have more likelihood of making satisfying choices if we have information. Knowledge is power.

WE'VE BEEN ROBBED: MOTHERHOOD LOST

Empowerment

Often when the topics discussed in this book arise, there is a quick jump to arguing about the rights of women. Sometimes in such debate the rights of women are pitted against those of their babies. Other times it becomes about the rights of women to pursue their lives. What about the rights of infant women; the rights of babies (newborn men and women)? We contend that the biological model of mothering allows everyone to win. On the surface, it may look as though a woman is being returned to a subservient role with such a model, but the reality is that in embracing motherhood she finds new strength, maturity, and great power as a woman, learning a multitude of new skills as she settles into the roles required to raise a child. In the biological model baby's needs are met and the expectations of a mother's biology are fulfilled. Even as they age, mothers reap benefits to their bodies and minds: better immune systems; fewer cancers, osteoporosis, and other age-related maladies; as well as lower rates of depression. Motherhood propels psychosocial development in an exquisite and unparalleled way.

It's hard to imagine how we've evolved a construct that doesn't honor motherhood, though often modern agendas are framed by such notions. Historically, the early champions for women were operating within a context that saw motherhood as a privilege, an honor worth protecting, acknowledging the obvious truth that motherhood is uniquely feminine. It's one thing that only women can accomplish.

Early feminists wrote about and argued these points. In today's climate, motherhood is perceived by many as something that gets in the way of living, an inconvenience that they want to "get out of the way." Such a statement stands in stark contrast to the woman who knows that she will grieve when her years of birthing are over. Unfortunately, the place of women, whether mothers or not, has been politicized to the point of making meaningful dialogue all but impossible.

In a February 2, 1909 public meeting, the question was asked, "Would there be sufficient protection for motherhood if women were in politics?" As women began to be included in the public experience, there was some legitimate concern over the very issues that are now at the heart of controversy one hundred years later. Unfortunately, we seemed to have stopped asking the questions about how motherhood would be affected by the myriad of choices for women liberated. Having women in the workplace is nothing new. What is new is that now these women leave their babies to strangers all day, rather than bringing them to work in a baby wrap of some kind.

Even today, most other cultures recognize the importance of reproduction. In some parts of the world, men can divorce women purely on the basis of "barrenness." In other cultures, the perky breasts that are valued in our culture are a sign of childlessness and their owners are pitied. Within many societies, women come into "power" only by becoming mothers. Going clear back to biblical times we see the anguish for women whose wombs were "closed," as well as the great exalting of those whose wombs were fruitful.

Ask any woman who is struggling with the deep pain of infertility about the importance of becoming a mother. She may feel safe enough to describe this most grievous anguish of her heart, the desperation and biological imperative she feels to experience the assumed right, responsibility, and great joy of having a child.

Once upon a time, the value and importance of motherhood was obvious to all people everywhere. Motherhood was revered, even held as sacred.

Consider these quotations:

I remember my mother's prayers and they have always followed me. They have clung to me all my life.

—Abraham Lincoln (1809–1865)

My mother was the most beautiful woman I ever saw. All I am I owe to my mother. I attribute all my success in life to the moral, intellectual and physical education I received from her.

—George Washington (1732–1799)

Of all the rights of women, the greatest is to be a mother.

—Lin Yutang

The heart of a mother is a deep abyss at the bottom of which you will always find forgiveness.

—Honore' de Balzac (1799–1850)

The mother's heart is the child's schoolroom.

—Henry Ward Beecher (1813–1887)

To understand a mother's love, bear your own children.

—Chinese Proverb

Alice Hawthorne

Who is it that loves me and will love me forever with an affection which no chance, no misery, no crime of mine can do away?—It is you, my mother.

—Thomas Carlyle

When God thought of mother, He must have laughed with satisfaction, and framed it quickly—so rich, so deep, so divine, so full of soul, power, and beauty, was the conception.

—Henry Ward Beecher

I think my life began with waking up and loving my mother's face.

—George Eliot

Mothers reflect God's loving presence on earth.

—William R. Webb

There is no friendship, no love, like that of the parent for the child.

—Henry Ward Beecher

Her children arise and call her blessed.

—Proverbs 31:28

A mother is the truest friend we have, when trials, heavy and sudden, fall upon us; when adversity takes the place of prosperity; when friends who rejoice with us in our sunshine, desert us when troubles thicken around us, still will she cling to us, and endeavor by her kind precepts and counsels to dissipate the clouds of darkness, and cause peace to return to our hearts.

—Washington Irving

Paradise lies at the feet of Mothers.

—Koran

Kids are not accessories to life. They are the life.

—Dr. Laura Schlessinger

The hand that rocks the cradle, rules the world.
Blessings on the hand of women!

—William Ross Wallace

When folding the American flag, each fold symbolizes a value. The ninth fold is a tribute to womanhood; for it has been through their faith, love, loyalty and devotion that the character of the men and women who have made this country great have been molded.[2]

The Mandarin Chinese character for "good" combines the characters for woman and child together - a woman tending a child as the epitome of "good."

Old World

Motherhood is the bridge between knowledge and wisdom.

—Lisa Marasco

Along the way as the 20th century gave way to more "modern" thinking, motherhood lost its place. Psychology and medicine had come up with a more sophisticated understanding of the world and it did not involve a warm view of mothering.

The convergence of medicine and psychology in this war on mother-baby love resulted in a deadly coup, from which we are still trying to recover.

In the early 1900's, mortality rates, especially for the young and elderly and even more so in foundling homes (or orphanages), were alarmingly high. In response, Dr. Luther E. Holt began using more isolation of patients in order to reduce transmission of germs. Around

2 www.usflag.org, US Air Force Academy

the same time, Psychologist Dr. John Watson was warning against mother-love and parental affection, admonishing parents not to exhibit any kind of "petting", hugging, kissing, and so on, though he did allow parents a good-night handshake or pat on the head.

Freud talked about the unique character of the tie between mother and child and at the same time taught that in the end, any maternal reality of that relationship is, in the experience of the child, trumped by whatever fantasy or interpretation is his. For instance, his mother may feel a great deal of love and commitment towards him, but if all he experiences is absence or harshness, he "feels unloved." Therefore, *what is and was in the child's mind* is what matters. Consequently, in Freud's thinking an absent mother can be replaced by an ever-present fantasy with no damage to either of them. I find this to be an ironic notion as it was Freud who also blamed many mental illnesses on dysfunctional mothering.

The final drain of modern mother-love remnants was completed by B.F. Skinner's proof of ability to shape any desired behavior, thereby adding credence to the notion that human beings, particularly the smaller ones, are little more than lumps of protoplasm to be shaped and reshaped at will. No longer did science view the baby as a little being with a spirit, in need of love and nurturing to form a healthy personality.

In the early twentieth century, Dr. Watson, a famous behavior specialist, filmed his experiments with a child, Little Albert. In these films, one sees a friendly, happy little boy reaching out to touch small animals. Each time Albert attempts to play with them a scary noise is sounded. By the end of the experiment, we see him crying and fearful at the mere sight of anything furry. How disturbing to watch the ease with which a young fragile personality is changed and damaged. Professional opinion was now firmly entrenched in the notion that babies did best in isolation, without affection and with proper rewards and punishments. Any question of who the caretaker was to be became patently irrelevant. Almost a century later, we still operate out of these ideas that have been disproven through a wide body of research. The 21st century has allowed us greater understanding through new research tools, yet our practices continue to be unconnected to new knowledge. As we will see below, more recent theory has given us much better understanding of human development, yet has not been connected to our current practices, which still reflect these disproven notions of Freud, Skinner, and others.

Then along came Rene' Spitz, James Robertson, Harry Harlow, and John Bowlby, to name a few other "experts." For the most part they stumbled onto their discoveries, which rocked the "knowledge" of the day as the 20th century neared its midpoint. Drs. Spitz and Robertson had been horrified to discover the blatant grief and apparent depression that young isolated children demonstrated (the term "hospitalized" had been coined for children traumatized by separation). They thought that if they produced film of these children people would be enlightened. Instead the researchers were accused of lacking academic integrity and were roundly criticized and dismissed.

Dr. Harlow may have stumbled upon the most incontrovertible, albeit methodologically controversial, evidence to shake the scientific community to its core. His famous wire-mother monkey experiments put the lie to the prevailing notion that babies need mother (or any caretaker) solely for the purposes of feeding. He had never intended to work with monkeys but found himself with a small lab in which monkeys were provided. He barely knew what he was looking for when he accidentally came upon the discovery that he could actually teach them how to use tools, solve puzzles, and so on, as it was "known for a fact" that monkeys were incapable of learning. And he was most definitely not trying to study love when he created his artificial mothers. Driven by funding problems, he was trying to breed his own supply of monkeys for further research and began to note problems in personality, behavior, learning ability, and more in his monkey babies, whom he kept in isolation, attempting to avoid transmission of disease. And so were born the famous experiments, as well as his own surprise at the discovery. A mother's love matters. Not the fantasy of it per Freud and not the germ-free cordiality of keeping children alive per Holt and Watson but the messy, mushy, warm power of a present, affectionate mother. He accomplished this in part by providing baby monkeys with two mothers: one, a soft terrycloth mother with no capacity for feeding; the other a cold mother made of wire but able to provide a bottle. He was astonished to discover that the babies only went to the wire mother when hungry, preferring to be "cuddled" and comforted by the soft mother. This was in direct opposition to Freud's thought. Harlow described the babies' need for their mothers as nothing short of "addiction."

"Addiction" has become a loaded term in our experience. We tend to think of an addict as someone passed out with a bottle in his hand or a needle in her arm. Yet, consider the dynamics of this. An addict is driven by desperation to once again feel comforted by his "high." There is little he won't do to achieve this. So it is with babies and their mothers. The word "addiction" is actually quite descriptive of the baby's need for Mother.

Harlow was roundly and soundly criticized by his colleagues, by animal rights groups, and by feminists everywhere. The content of his discovery was—and is—often ignored because of the discomfort of his monkeys while he studied them.

Fortunately his work was bolstered by the concurrent research of John Bowlby and some of Bowlby's students, such as Mary Ainsworth. They were making the same discoveries with human children in various contexts. It is an interesting side note that when Dr. Bowlby visited Dr. Harlow, years after Dr. Harlow had described and demonstrated the acute need of a baby for his mother, it was Dr. Bowlby who pointed out that perhaps it would be better if the mother and infant monkeys were not placed in separate cages from each other as was Harlow's habit, but rather kept together as a unit.

By the time the Sixties were coming to a close, there was a new focus on love and relationships in Western culture. One has to wonder if the "All you need is love" generation was prompted by its own lack of parental affection, having been raised a la Skinner et al. Nonetheless this new generation of parents was seemingly more aware of the needs of their babies for love, touch, and attention than its grandparents had been.

It's all about relationship!

Just as the baby is "addicted" by love for his mother, mothers who are well bonded through breastfeeding and continuous holding, touch, and other nurturing behaviors often describe a positive, happy, wonderful addiction to the baby. This longing to be constantly together is short-lived, gradually giving way to different experiences as the child grows. Our culture dictates such things as "date night" or "second honeymoon" without baby along, though most of these mothers find such separations to be exquisitely painful. The "date" is often spent talking about the baby, longing for him, worrying whether or not he is all right as all the while her leaking breasts create interesting new patterns on her expensive blouse.

Many mothers of babies deeply desire for their partners to welcome the fullness of parenthood and longing to be in proximity just as the mothers do. In his book *The Seven Principles for Making Marriage Work*, Dr. John M. Gottman makes the point that in a successful marriage the husband has to transition from longing for the couple's old "normal" relationship to understanding and embracing the "new normal" that Baby brings—embracing it fully, just as his wife has. A quality I most deeply appreciate in my husband is his talent as a dad and the knowledge that he is the one person who loves my babies as much as I do. This has added an unparalleled dimension of strength in our marriage. My friend Laura Alexander once said in a lecture, "The biggest turn-on for me is watching my husband coach our boys in a baseball game." Clearly, things are different in a marriage once children are added! Dr. William Sears writes in several of his books about the importance of the father's role in attaching to Baby and supporting his wife's efforts in mothering as a great opportunity to experience happiness.

Much changed over the second half of the twentieth century. Our problems now seem to be bigger and more complex: rampant divorce; children being raised by single parents who may be doing the best that they can but are often stretched beyond reasonable emotional and financial limits; children engaging in sexual experimentation at younger and younger ages; drug use, abuse, and addictions skyrocketing and starting at younger ages—our societal fabric being torn at by many novel concerns tearing at it.

In this new century we seem to be characterized by relationships that are temporary and replaceable. One entertainer, commenting on a six-year marriage that had ended, described that relationship as a great success, with the most longevity of all relationships he'd had. Online dating services and electronic interactions allow people to fall in and out of love with people they've never shared physical space with—sometimes on the other side of the world!

While correlation most certainly does not prove causation, it would be unwise not to consider one of the big changes since the last century—how babies are birthed and then routinely separated from mothers starting just as the baby is trying to cope with the commotion of the delivery room and then continuing throughout his infancy and young childhood. This separation of mothers and babies in the early years is an unprecedented social experiment. Our modern birth experience separates the mother and baby into cold individual compartments, often devoid of the hormones biologically mandated for their survival. Oxytocin, the primary "love chemical" known to facilitate bonding, is released with touch, necessitating presence. Separation damages this system, leaving relational deficits that we are only beginning to understand.

Genetic changes continue as we maneuver our way through the third generation of the grand experiment of artificially feeding infants. Never before in history have such a sizeable group of women left their babies for such a large portion of each day. Add to that the fact that babies are also contending with some of the problems mentioned above (i.e. relational problems between their parents, etc.) and it would appear that there is great reason for concern, if not downright alarm.

While it would be an improper goal to have children for our own selfish ends, the reality is that often our own immersion into motherhood is a transforming experience, one that heals much that is hurting in our own attachment history. When we discuss "attachment history" we are referring to our own security in loving relationships (or lack thereof). Sadly, many mothers are denied this immersion either by their choice or by their ignorance, or sometimes by necessity to be away from baby, thereby missing out on the intense attachment and bonding once expected in motherhood. Our society has so diluted the role and experience of "mother" that we can barely conceive of a model of immersion, finding the idea to be an impossible inconvenience. Yet our biological state requires it for our optimal health.

In Swahili there are no separate words for "mother" and "baby," but rather "mamatoto" to describe the inseparable dyad. The idea is that though birth has begun the separation of the two, it will be some time before more independence is desirable.

The experience of mothering may be essential to the development of the adult woman as well. According to Erik Erikson, women successfully complete the stage known as "generativity versus stagnation" through motherhood or a reasonable facsimile such as teaching or some other form of nurturing. Erikson describes the experience of having children as a strong prompt to complete development as an adult; the demands of caring for another assist us in leaving our immaturity behind. For most the surest way out of self-absorption is to become a parent.

Once, while preparing a lecture on parenting, I asked thirty or forty men and women about how they had been changed by becoming parents. While there were a multitude of divergent and interesting responses, there was one answer given by *every* participant. "I'm not as selfish anymore."

Birth is—and perhaps was designed to be—the beginning of the transformational experience of the new role as Mother. When I was growing up my grandmother told me her birth stories over and over, weaving her joy and pain into the fabric of each event, creating a vivid picture of her babies' arrivals. Her unfailing reference to these stories demonstrates the truth that birth is perhaps the most profound experience that we may encounter in our lifetime. Those of us who experienced natural births are often so thrilled by it that we tell—and retell—the story to anyone who stands still long enough! Now, women are bypassing the whole experience of laboring and pushing babies out, sensations removed by medications or sometimes preferring the "superiority" of having their babies removed from them surgically.

It has been known for some time that epidurals inhibit the release of oxytocin, the hormone that promotes and facilities bonding and attachment, among other things. Additionally, the pressure of the baby's head on the vaginal walls stimulates the largest release of this important hormone of a woman's lifetime, an advantage missed when the baby is removed through surgery and does not pass through the birth canal. This hormone must be released this way for a reason, and indeed we know that this primes both the mother and the baby for the bonding and attachment process to begin momentarily. Does that mean that mothers who have scheduled c-sections don't love their babies? Of course not! It is interesting to note, however, that many women who have had both natural births and births with high intervention speak longingly and sadly about the difference in the bonds with the children. This difference seems to remain over years, not just in the moments after birth.

It has been a sad notation for those of us who work with child-bearing families that, since the advent of epidurals and the "too posh to push" mentality, we hear birth stories much less frequently than we once did. Where previously women came in contact with new empowerment and excitement over what they were capable of, birth is now often described in terms that fall under "just another day at the office" or something so horrible that "I just wanted to get it over with." Many of the younger women in our culture will never know the joy of that birth transformation, nor will they even know that they are missing anything.

A significant change in birthing practices occurred in recent history, when the responsibility for birth left the hands of women, often friends or family, and moved into the formal medical arena of mostly male strangers. This has happened over such a period of time that most of us who are living now have no other lens through which to view and evaluate it. We tend to evaluate our experience for the most part with a sweeping statement, such as, "Well, I was born that way and I turned out ok," similar to, "I eat junk food and I'm healthy." My grandfather said, "I smoked for sixty years and it didn't hurt me any." In Grandpa's case, that seemed to be true--until he developed the cancer that killed him.

The problem with these assessments is that we have no ability to do a comparison. I can't possibly know how much healthier I would or would not have been had I been born differently, breastfed longer, parented another way, and so forth. Yet there is ample research with hard data that points to the conclusion that I could have been healthier, physically and emotionally, had my parents and health care providers known differently.

Consider the changes in four generations of mothers. My grandmother had two homebirths with her midwife-aunt, in the 1930s. Ten years later, she experienced two hospital births with a friendly doctor and not-so-friendly nurses. These experiences were so very powerfully positive and negative respectively that when she was in her 80s and becoming demented she could still recount the stories and the emotions surrounding them, better than she could recite the names of those babies. My mother, a well-educated woman had wanted to have a natural birth in the 50s because she had read the book, *Childbirth Without Fear* by Dr. Grandly Dick-Read. This book discusses the benefits of sparing the mother and baby from the harmful effects of drugs used in childbirth. However, finding a doctor to "allow" this was impossible at the time. (I was one of a rare group of babies born in the 50s with my father in attendance, however! He told the doctor, "I'm paying for it and I'm going to watch.") Twenty-two years later, when I gave birth the first time I was able to find a doctor who "allowed" me to have more, albeit still limited, choices about my experience. Mine was the first "Lamaze all the Way!" birth in that hospital, and they were so excited, they invited the staff in to witness. Another twenty-five years and I looked around to see women voluntarily abdicating their choices in favor of the medical establishment's provision of epidurals, inductions, and Cesarean Sections; all driven by money and fear. The first "liberated" generation of women seemingly gave away all power and control over this momentous physical, emotional, and spiritual event. Ironically, the recipients of this power-abdication were primarily men in the medical establishment.

Can we see a disconnect here?

Women are less "allowed" to have the births they want than ever, birth plans and childbirth education notwithstanding. One doctor told me that he practiced in ways that he knew were sub-optimal for women because of the lawyers breathing down his neck. Astoundingly, we now see women choosing a surgical delivery with the "too posh to push" phenomenon. It was with great joy that I "caught" my grandchildren as my daughter chose to be in control of her births, a rarity in today's generation of birthing women. She experienced wonderful, midwife-attended births for which she became an advocate but is often viewed with suspicion by friends and strangers alike.

Women are brainwashed from their earliest years to believe that somehow birth in a hospital with a doctor is the only safe way to have a baby. Her own pleasure in the event must be set aside for the presumption of safety. Yet there is no research to date that validates these myths for healthy, normal, low-risk pregnancy and birth. Is there any truth to the idea that she must give up the joy so that she and the baby will be "safe"?

Similarly, infant formula makers have spent billions of dollars to convince us from our childhood that their product is better than what God designed. Baby dolls for toddlers are sold with bottles and pacifiers so that this little girl learns to "mother-by-plastic." When breastfeeding is written about in most media pieces, it is viewed as a sacrifice that most women can't possibly make, certainly not for any reasonable length of time. The horror stories of failed attempts are paraded out as if they are the rule, rather than the exception. Professionals who support breastfeeding, such as lactation consultants, are often pinned with nicknames such as "nipple Nazis." Our breasts are pervasively pictured, used to sell everything from workbooks to motorcycles, and referred to and degraded as nothing more than men's toys instead of the beautifully designed baby feeders that they are designed to be. Public nursing is often viewed with revulsion. How often do we hear about the joy, wonder, and supremacy of the maternal experience of nursing a baby?

Women who decide to nurse babies—and especially those who, often to the chagrin of those around them, decide to nurse them longer than a few weeks—have to put up with barriers imposed by employers, teachers, institutions, and all manner of social commentary often spoken in incredibly rude tones and verbiage seemingly reserved for these women alone.

One woman with a newborn was at a popular Los Angeles museum for a day out, shortly after the funeral of her two-year-old daughter. She was obviously grieving and in a raw emotional state. Her baby began to fuss, so she chose a quiet, out-of-the-way corner to nurse her. An older woman spotted her, made a disgusting face and shouted something about her not doing THAT, before beating a hasty retreat behind a door. This poor mother was devastated. Had she been on a beach showing much more of her breasts to many more people, this beautiful woman would have been celebrated.

When we embrace our new role it begins to also become our identity. This is sometimes viewed in a negative light. We are so avidly determined to be "individuals" that we sometimes have a tendency to "throw the baby out with the bathwater." Perhaps there would be joy in embracing an identity that is tied to another human being. In a column written for *Newsweek*, Anna Quindlen poignantly writes of her soon-to-be empty nest. She talks of raising her children as her refrigerator magnet announces, "Mom is not my real name." As her essay concludes with her now-grown children's exits from the home, she proudly proclaims, "Mom *is* my real name. It is, it is."[3]

---

3 **"Flown Away Left Behind", Anna Quindlen, 2004**

Time was, not so long ago, when little girls planned and dreamed of becoming mothers. They looked forward to it and prepared for it by playing with dolls (or with younger siblings if they were lucky enough to have them), babysitting, and taking "home economics" classes. The happy expectation was that, after high school, they would step into adulthood and the expectations of marriage and children. Most first babies were born by the mothers' mid-twenties at the latest.

Biology drives survival and reproduction. The drive to reproduce begins at puberty. All biological entities have two requirements: to survive and to reproduce. For the first time in history, we have the ability to circumvent the second demand of biology. We now often have at least a fifteen-year gap between puberty and marriage, followed by more time passing before reproduction. One of many negative results is an ever-increasing rate of breast cancer. Texts on human lactation consistently include research on breast cancer, demonstrating such things as age of first birth as a critical factor, with younger ages providing better protection, but this receives little publicity

The current "girls just wanna have fun" notion that pervades the Millennial Generation may in fact turn out to be to their great detriment, as they turn off natural instincts to partner and reproduce in favor of less meaningful sexual and relational pursuits. Perhaps that is a partial explanation for the ever-lengthening time to complete brain development. Having fun would not propel development in the same manner as having adult responsibilities, particularly parenthood.

We may be pouring fuel onto the fire of denying the power of *mamatoto* by the way we talk about breastfeeding. Even advocates such as lactation consultants often see the product (milk) as the important part of the equation, ignoring the process (intimacy, nurturing, comfort, attachment, etc.). Often if the baby receives breastmilk out of a bottle, he is still viewed as a breastfed baby. While breastmilk via any delivery system is better than formula, this idea denies the very critical realities of what happens to promote attachment at the breast during the process of feeding and stands in direct conflict with Attachment Theory.

La Leche League, a support group for breastfeeding mothers which grew into a world-renowned authority on human lactation, was founded by seven mothers who met together to help one another figure out how to reclaim successful breastfeeding during a time when new formulas were being developed and promoted as science's improvement over God and nature. One of these remarkable women, Edwina Froelich, told the story of her pregnancy at a conference where I was also speaking. She recounted that during a time when women were condescended to and patronized, told to just "leave everything to the doctor", she dared to ask her doctor about her pregnancy. She said her doctor seemed excited to share information with her, climbed up to the top shelf of his bookcase, chose a book, blew the dust off the top, and proceeded to open to her "the secrets of the uterus".

It is difficult now to understand how shocking this was. People didn't talk about such things at that time. The word "pregnancy" wasn't used in polite company and women and men did not discuss things anatomical. La Leche League was so named because the local paper would not allow advertisements for meetings with the word "breastfeeding" in it. When my grandma became pregnant for the first time and queried female relatives about how the baby would get out, she was met with stern, knowing looks accompanied by, "You'll see."

Now we find ourselves in a time and place that is rich with information and options, a time when open discussion is welcome and women have more cultural equality than at any other time and place in history. We can access information on any topic at any time without leaving our homes. My children could discuss the wonder of birth before they went to preschool. Yet we ignore what is known, trying to create some new truth, whether it matches the hard realities of biology or not. The "secrets of the uterus" are taken for granted to the point of being ignored.

At what point will women decide to step into their rightful place of power over their bodies and babies? What is it that causes otherwise strong, bright women to cast aside their control of this amazingly profound event?

While I have great respect for skilled doctors of both genders and gratefulness for the specialized abilities of OB-GYNs to assist in the pregnancies and births that include complications making them dangerous to mother or baby, most births don't require such trained assistance. While some men are very sympathetic and kind during labor, the reality is that a man can't ever know the sensation of a contraction or the exquisite pain of the baby's tongue moving against a nipple abrasion. Mothers are the only ones who know. Therefore, while men may indeed be a critical part of a given birth experience, it may be that women have much better outcomes when there is also female support, such as a loving mother, sister, friend, doula[4], or midwife.

Down the road, when problems occur, we don't necessarily connect the dots in a way that allows us to see their genesis. For example, there is good data that some forms of leukemia are much more common in children who were not breastfed for a substantial amount of time. It would seem unlikely that parents would question early feeding practices while in the midst of a dread diagnosis and treatment. Doctors would not insensitively say at that point, "Well, this is somewhat avoidable by breastfeeding long term." So, the connection is not made in people's minds, despite proof provided by research. Ignorance sustained by denial allows us to continue avoiding the truth.

Breast cancer studies have shown that more total months of breastfeeding, especially when combined with younger childbearing, confer significant risk-reduction for breast cancer—both for

---

4 A doula is a professional Labor Assistant. She often teaches an expectant couple as they learn about healthy birth and then attends the big event supporting both the mother and her partner. Often she interprets and advocates for the couple with the medical system when questions arise.

the breastfed baby girl and for the mother herself. Yet these studies are often met with dismissive comments such as, "How can we ask a woman to do that?" and, "This data includes unrealistic demands." Time and again we have studies showing various cancer risk reduction around early childbearing and breastfeeding, yet because that flies in the face of a woman's "right" to a fulfilling career, this information is often withheld or reported in a derisive way, allowing for easy dismissal.

We act as if we can—or should—change biology just because we don't like the way it works. Evidence tells us that our children need long-term breastfeeding, yet we behave as if we can simply bypass that information and there will be no consequence. It's doubtful that any one will learn from my bottle fed step-granddaughter's lifelong battle with painful eczema. She is viewed with great sympathy and no lessons taken. Most of the people in her life don't understand the evidence connecting formula to eczema, diabetes, Crohn's disease, some childhood cancers, and a long list of other maladies. How does the mother's right to choose formula win out over the lifetime of potential suffering for her asthmatic or diabetic child?

Recently, a television documentary explored the terrible pain and difficulty that goes into a decision about an unplanned pregnancy. The couple being described already had a baby and found themselves pregnant again soon after. Many of the complex issues were detailed and we could feel the angst of this couple. One who understands the research on breastfeeding can't help but think that all of this hardship could have likely been avoided if the mother had been assisted and supported in breastfeeding, thereby naturally delaying her fertility.

Occasionally, someone makes remarks about our ability to manipulate biology through technology. An example would be our ability to accomplish in-vitro fertilization. The point is also sometimes made that our new technological society is rewiring brains, so obviously biology can be modified. Perhaps this is our way of staying in a state of denial about the damage we may be doing and the inevitable tipping point. And even if it is accurate that our technological society is rewiring brains, who are we trusting to decide in what ways our brains should be altered?

In spite of such a backdrop, we in our current culture seem to have lost sight of biological realities. When modern feminism began to take the stage, it was common to hear comments from the movement such as, "Being home all day with little children is incredibly boring." One has to wonder if perhaps the attachment process was short-circuited, perhaps by bottle-feeding or other suboptimal practices. Otherwise, it seems like a non sequitur to talk about one's "addiction" or love object as a daily and boring burden.

Could it be that the generation that made these statements was "bored" due to being disconnected from their children and unable to experience the reward and joy of a connected relationship with the children they are caring for? Perhaps this problem has its roots with "modern" practices of drugged births and bottle-feeding, not to mention the quick succession of more babies that is ameliorated by absence of fertility during the early months of breastfeeding for most women?

It is a mistake to assume in our research that breastfeeding babies are the same as bottle-feeding ones, that nursing mothers are the same as bottle-feeding mothers, and that the relationships formed in these very different contexts would be comparable. Making them equivalent becomes the quintessential "apples and oranges" discussion. The fact that we tend to see these babies as the same is, in and of itself, a commentary on how much we are missing the boat.

Perhaps the experience of *mamatoto* is so dramatically different that the immersed mother, while often tired and stressed by her full-time job of parenting, would also not refer to her life as "boring." Maybe she has found other "professional mothers" to enjoy community with. Likely she has continually educated herself, enriching her mind. Possibly she has found a way to weave career into her mothering without sacrificing the quality of her nurturing.

Her baby's milk-dribbling smile provides her with a sense of joy, the strength of which is deeply satisfying in a way that surprises her. Who knew that something as simple as this smile gives her a sense of purpose as she is reminded that what she is doing will have untold impact on society in the future? How she loves and treats this baby will have impact on his contributions to the world years later. This baby's needs, right here, right now, on this day are being attended to.

The rituals just seemed to stop, like all other natural endings-such as the last time one of the boys crawled into bed with us, or I carried them on my hips, or saw them naked, even. Such moments evaporate so quietly that you don't realize it's the last time until long afterward[5].

GRANDMOTHER BROWN'S HUNDRED YEARS

1827-1927a

[An illustration of traditional mothering practices.]

Whatever the work to be carried through to
completion, whether for the dead or the living,
one's children must not be neglected.

Gus used to follow me around sometimes,
those first years on the farm, saying doggedly,
"Mother! Mother! I've got me some tiredness,
I want to be took [i.e., taken up and nursed]."
Poor little fellow!

It seemed as if the only time when I felt
justified in taking up a book or paper was when
I sat down to nurse my babies. I always nursed
them till they were pretty big. I couldn't bear
to wean them, they kept so fat and pretty as
long as I fed them at the breast. And so it
happened that Frank would sometimes pull at

5 *A Year by the Sea: Thoughts of an Unfinished Woman*, **Joan Anderson**

my skirt and hand me a newspaper, as a hint that he would like to be taken up and nursed.

Herbert declares he can remember the last time I nursed him, and perhaps he can, for it was the only way I could quiet and comfort him. It was one day long after he had been weaned and was running around independently in house and garden, when a bee stung him. (I was stung by a bald hornet once, and I never had anything hurt me so much in all my life as that did.)

Anyway, for many years all my household tasks were performed with an ear cocked for the cry of a waking baby. How often I used to think what happiness it would be if I had nothing to do except take care of my babies!

One morning, it was the fifth day of May, 1888 he went away, my last baby. I stood at the door to watch him go down the street. I cannot tell you how I felt. It was a lovely spring morning, but I felt as if the end of the world had come. No children in my home any more! The last one going from me. Oh, oh, oh! And yet I would not have held him back.

Harriet Connor Brown, Grandmother Brown's Hundred Years: 1827-1927 (NewYork: BlueRibbonBooks)

BRAVE NEW TECHNO WORLD

BY NANCY WILLIAMS

Almost a hundred years after these new ideas began to take place, on the heels of many cultural changes in expectation; I was working my way through college, often earning extra money by house-sitting, which sometimes included watching children. I took care of a favorite baby for much of his first year, usually for weekends at a time. When his parents returned after a weekend camping trip, I excitedly told them, "Nicky learned to crawl!" The mother slumped against the wall, slid to the floor. Through her tears she repeated, "I missed it. I missed it." Her grief over missing an important rite of motherhood was a normal response to her instincts, her mother's heart trying to function in a context that denies both.

This is a good thing for women?

We are in the midst of one of the largest experiments ever done on human subjects. The biology of birth and necessary early care of humans hasn't changed, and yet in less than a century we have seriously altered the context in which this occurs. The long-term consequences are only beginning to be seen.

Not to worry—a student recently explained that we can now violate biology with impunity because medicine is advanced enough to deal with any consequences. Tell that to the woman who waited too long and now can't conceive and has no money for alternative treatments. And be sure and share that with parents while their baby is in the emergency room with a life-threatening illness which could have been prevented by following the biological imperative to breastfeed.

Recent research is showing unexpected biophysical components of motherhood. When women are pregnant, the baby releases some of his stem cells into her bloodstream. These releases occur at various times during the pregnancy, with a large burst shortly before birth. One has to wonder if that process may be short-circuited with inductions or C-sections. While it is still unproven how these stem cells are used, what is known is that they will circulate through the mother's bloodstream for many years. The theory is that the mother's body uses them to enhance her immune system.

It is now also know that the mother's brain changes dramatically when she gives birth.

> *New research indicates that the dramatic hormonal fluctuations that occur during pregnancy, birth and lactation may remodel the female brain, increasing the size of the neurons in some regions and producing structural changes in others.* (Kinsley and Lambert, Scientific American, 2006)

The left brain hemisphere of a new mother is a bit foggy as it "writes down what you say." The right brain, more active in new mothers, remembers words associated with strong emotion. Certainly delivery of the baby and the weeks following are filled with intense emotion. The right brain keeps us living in the moment, focusing in on the constant needs of an infant. The infant himself is right brain-dominant until age three.

According to Dr. Allan Schore in a remark made at a seminar for therapists, most babies prefer the mother's left breast, which in most mothers is the best producer. When the baby is nursing on the mother's left side in the most common cradle hold, the mother is gazing into his left eye, stroking the left side of his body, and the sounds would be more distinct in his left ear. All of this is then directed to and processed by the right brain—exactly where the baby has his primary experiences.

Mothers who are not comfortable in their right brains may have more difficulty, as mothering behavior is in large part instinctual, rather than analytical. It is common to hear mothers discuss their difficulties in ignoring their hearts in favor of complying with some "expert" and the dogma of the day. ***A well-attached mother is the best expert on her child that there is.***

What can we say of the hormones of mothering? These complex, interactive chemicals cause us to be more patient, relaxed, nurturing, responsive, and in general more loving women. These heightened emotional states are not restricted to our response to our nursing babies, but also impact our response to the rest of the world around us. One could speculate on the impact to society when women as a group are not experiencing the chemical state once considered to be normal and expected, especially when the hormones in questions are those that support relationships, community, marriage, friendships, some careers, and the like. Perhaps this has led to a culture that is not quite as gentle as it once was.

Maternal hormones play another important role for mothers: they stave off depression. Just a generation ago, true postpartum depression and other mood disorders related to parturition were rare events. Not to be confused with the more common "baby blues," true depression is debilitating. An interesting theory suggests that, based on research showing a higher rate of depression in the absence of breastfeeding or with premature weaning, the mother's body may be biologically determined to "grieve," to feel terrible sadness if lactation does not occur or is not happening properly.

In the most severe cases, depression can devolve into psychosis. In less dramatic instances, it often interferes with attachment and bonding. A myriad of studies has demonstrated the harmful effects of depression on the mother-baby relationship. This is especially troubling in light of the fact that the baby of a mother prone to depression is born with a higher genetic risk for his/her own depressive problems. A secure attachment would ameliorate this higher risk but if the mother displays poor emotional expression, she has a more difficult time developing a connection with the baby. Many of these mothers find themselves incapacitated on the most basic levels—unable to care for the family or house, or even to get out of bed. In depressed moms, a change is observed in the infants' EEG, matching that of the mother. (Field, Fox, Pickens, Nawrock, 1995) There are also statistically higher rates in the incidence of Sudden Infant Death Syndrome with maternal depression. (Mitchell, et al, 2008)

Unfortunately, it is not uncommon for well-meaning health care providers to insist on immediate weaning when a woman is seeking care for her depression. Several incorrect assumptions may be at play here. First, because of our culture's confusion about the nature of mothering relationships, it is often taken for granted that it will be a kindness to take the baby from the mother and relieve her of his care. Let's examine this. Mother is already feeling a sense of sadness and loss, as well as inadequacy. Perhaps she is struggling with a less-than-satisfying birth experience, even to the point of qualifying for a post traumatic stress disorder diagnosis, which is happening more and more frequently. What message may she receive as we inadvertently imply that others can take better care of her baby than she can? Additionally, we are heaping more loss onto her experience with the separation from her baby. A common remark made by mothers whose babies have been in hospital nurseries or otherwise away from the mother's side is, "I couldn't sleep at all. I was constantly missing my baby and worried about how he was."

Another reason given for immediate weaning is so that Mom can take medication. This is simply absurd given the various medication options available today. Many, many medications in most classes of drugs are considered compatible with breastfeeding. Some may require monitoring of the baby's serum levels, but even at that one has to ask: how safe is it to take the baby off the breast? It is a known fact that the hormonal chaos of abrupt weaning may in and of itself trigger postpartum depression (Bowles et al, 2003). If postpartum depression is already at play, the weaning may seriously exacerbate the existing symptoms. If Mother is incapacitated yet still responsible for running the household, the times she sits with the baby to nurse may in fact be her only times of warm interaction and rest. Bottles can be propped. If she is so debilitated that she must be supervised, still she and the baby will do well to continue nursing. Cutting edge inpatient programs recognize this and maintain the breastfeeding relationship, either through rooming in or through frequent visits, facilitated by the father or other family or friends.

There is no such thing as a completely safe drug for anyone at any time. Each individual has the potential for a reaction with any drug or surgical procedure, which is why we give informed consent before receiving medical treatment. A person with no history of drug allergies can have a serious reaction even to penicillin. My grandfather died of a reaction to a local anesthetic while having a "safe, routine" operation. That said, most of the "risks" inherent in using medication during breastfeeding are theoretical and not borne out by research. At the same time, there is a wide body of research demonstrating serious risk when weaning is instituted early.

How will weaning impact the baby's experience? The current recommendations about duration of breastfeeding are a minimum of two years (World Health Organization) and a minimum of one year (American Academy of Pediatrics). The development of sound mental health includes secure attachment, but there is more and more evidence that formula threatens this health as well. Additionally, there is a long list of illnesses and other physical problems known to be associated with formula use—even one bottle. (See "Just One Bottle", page XX). Not only will the baby/child/adult be more likely to struggle with illness, some quite serious, but a sick child makes parenting much more difficult, leaving the mother and child with heightened vulnerabilities.

Additionally, abrupt weaning and/or separation of the dyad could have a serious impact on the family dynamics, impacting all those who care for him or interact with him, such as his father, grandmother, or aunt. With the co-opting of maternal tasks, these family members are now also feeding and caring for the baby. While in the short term that may not seem to matter, over the long haul it can stress the marriage and allow Mom to continue to withdraw from all things relational. Buying formula adds financial stress to a young family who by definition are struggling anyway. To make matters worse, the risk is high for yet another pregnancy. If they are under pressure with the current situation, imagine how hard it is to have *two* babies under the age of one or two!

Often, the mother's depression occurs in the context of two critical stressors: she finds herself isolated and she is trying to do too much. Here is a typical phone call from a mother in this situation: "I think I'm depressed. My baby is two weeks old. I have a one year-old, and a five-year old. My husband is in the military and we are moving this weekend. The last two days I went back to finish my work before we move and I've been helping my best friend who's getting divorced."

Somehow in this equation breastfeeding gets targeted as the reason she is overwhelmed. If she weans and now has to purchase artificial infant milk (formula), prepare and store bottles, warm a bottle while trying to attend to a hungry and crying baby, wash and sterilize bottles, etc., will her load be any less difficult to bear? Instead, she will be deprived of the necessary hormonal and chemical support for physical and mental health *and* saddled with the extra time, energy, and money required for artificial feeding.

One of the best things about being women is that we tend to be a little more skilled than men at creating friendships and community, possibly because we are more acutely attuned to our need for these relationships. Yet, we often choose loneliness when it comes to our new mothering role. This is sad and unnecessary. Women all over the world have access to other women who can mentor and teach, support, assist, commiserate, laugh, and cry together. These women can be found in faith communities, La Leche League, homeschool or PTA groups, Mom's Club or Mothers of Preschoolers groups, neighborhoods, and many other places. If worse comes to worse, communities can be created online, though one could question whether that is adequate for the kind of support one might find herself needing. The support found in online communities, while not enough on its own, can bolster a mother's spirits and is available any time night or day.

Even when there is no postpartum depression present, mothering young children is a full time, all-encompassing endeavor which can be referred to as "immersion." It is by far the most rewarding and joyous experience that one can have. It is also the most intense, difficult, and challenging. Oftentimes it stretches us to limits that we didn't know we were capable of, yet isn't that what often leads to growth? Having communities of support means that we have safe people around who will challenge us to grow and continue when it would be easier to give up. Many women choose to return to careers rather than motherhood, saying, "Work is easier." Perhaps, but is it better for anybody?

Rather, it may be helpful to hear how community support positively impacts a mother's experience, as told by Shawn Crane.

> *My dear friend Leigh is the mother of four children. She and her husband decided to add to their family by adopting. She was notified that a baby was available and needed to be placed in the next two days. Knowing that she is prone to following her heart and afraid that she might let her love of a darling baby overshadow good decision-making, Leigh asked me to come with her to meet the birth mother and baby. We met with the mother, and after asking a number of questions Leigh and Scott quickly decided that they were willing to take the baby. That evening Leigh's family and a number of others gathered at my house for a casual celebratory dinner. Realizing that supplies were needed for their new arrival Leigh decided to go on a quick shopping trip. A good friend offered to accompany her, and the next thing we knew a vanload of children decided to help as well. While Leigh and her friend shopped for diapers, clothing, and a few essentials my oldest son and his friends did a survey of infant car seats. By the time Leigh came to that area of the store they were able to give her a full report on the features and benefits of each. Leigh and company came back to my home and we discussed how best to support the family in welcoming their new addition.*

At nine o'clock the next morning, the baby was in their custody and would remain so for the next six weeks as the adoption was to be finalized. Leigh's family is a part of our homeschooling community, and the day she picked up the baby was the same day that we met for classes. She came directly to our meeting place and baby was welcomed literally with the open of arms of a dozen mothers, as well as children from the ages of six through eighteen. All wanted a turn holding him. I was lucky enough to have him stay with me while Leigh ran a quick errand. I held Baby nestled in a sling as I taught a writing class to one of his new sisters and a group of other children. A friend took Leigh to get a breast pump. Leigh is a strong breastfeeding advocate, and she was dedicated to breastfeeding this baby as she had her others. She was eager to get started building her milk supply. The rest of the day was spent playing "pass the baby please". We have a wonderful set of pictures of Baby being held by a loving community.

A few weeks after Baby arrived, the adoption social worker, knowing how taxing a newly adopted baby can be, expressed concern for Leigh and Scott. She wanted to know if they had any support from any friends or family. Most of their family lives far away, so she asked if they had friends who could offer help or support. Leigh responded by saying that her washing machine had been broken for the last 5 days and that two friends had been doing laundry for their family of 7 including the cloth diapers. She also mentioned that friends had been rotating bringing her family dinner every night for the last couple of weeks since Baby had arrived and were scheduled to continue doing so for as long as she felt the need. She went on to tell the social worker how other friends had been chauffeuring her older children around to various lessons and activities, another friend had made a run to the local farmer's market to pick up fresh produce for her family for the week, and that a baby shower was planned to officially welcome him to the community. She stopped speaking because she realized that the social worker was no longer listening. She just sat staring. When Leigh questioned her reaction she said with astonishment, "People have been bringing you dinner every night for the last two weeks?!" She claimed she had never heard of anything like that.

When Leigh told me that story, I was reminded again how unique our community appears to those who don't belong to such a group of women. This is a group of friends who have supported each other with practical and emotional help for many years. We have been with each other through wonderful and painful times alike. We've walked each other through marital conflicts, struggles with our children and fears about their well-being. We've supported each other through the deaths of parents, the heart attacks of spouses, frightening medical diagnoses for loved ones, and many other life-altering events. We each give to the others, and we have confidence that we will be on the receiving end of that love and support when life throws a challenge our way. We have watched older children while mom was in labor with a new sibling, brought meals, purchased groceries, delivered flowers and picked up dry cleaning. We have shared our various medical experiences, offered a shoulder to cry on and provided a listening ear. We have laughed together, read books together, camped together, traveled to seminars together, cried together, agonized and worried together, held each other up when things are tough and made a deal that we can't all being having a life crisis on the same day. We love each other, enjoy each other, and sometimes get angry with each other, but we are always willing to run an errand, care for a child, or rise to the occasion when support is needed.

There is an indelible snapshot in my mind of the nature of the relationship of this group of women. The birth mother of the baby that Leigh was adopting has a serious mental condition. Because of this, she was considered unfit for motherhood and Child Protective Services insisted she adopt the baby out or place him in foster care. Two days before the adoption was to be final Leigh received a call that there had been some glitch with the paperwork and due to this glitch there was nothing preventing the birth mother from having the baby returned to her. The mother insisted that the baby come back. After ten weeks of breastfeeding, caring for, and loving this baby, Leigh and her family had to return him to his birth mother. Leigh was devastated and sobbed through her phone call to me. I asked how I could help and she said, "I can't do this alone." We established a phone tree and when Leigh and her family arrived at the home of the birth mother the next morning there were friends there to walk her through the pain and difficulty of returning him. Mothers, fathers, and children, each a friend of Leigh and Scott or their children all gathered across the street from the home of the birth mother. In all, 40 people came to say goodbye to Baby and to support Leigh and her family as they walked through what will undoubtedly be one of the most painful day of their lives.

With a sense of sad irony we all returned to my home, the same home in which the baby shower had been held to celebrate his entering into Leigh's family. Now we met to mourn the loss of his inclusion in their family and our community. Leigh and Scott and their older children were held as they cried. Her younger ones were keep entertained and were watched over as they played. Since then Leigh has been the recipient of more dinners, loving phone calls and much love and support in general.

We cannot get through life without experiencing painful situations. Marriages crumble. Illness and tragedy strike parents, friends, spouses, and children. We cannot avoid pain in life but we need never walk through it alone if we take the time to find, build, and participate in community.

Many women, especially those who have spent years in a workplace environment, don't know how to find or build such a community. La Leche League, Mommy & Me classes, parks, community centers, religious communities, etc. all provide opportunities to find like-minded friends and fellow parents. Following a monthly meeting, a woman came up to me and asked, "I was wondering if you would like to get together to have lunch sometime because... well, frankly, I like you." We met for lunch that day and a nineteen year friendship ensued. Sometimes it really is that simple. Look for like-minded women, look for established groups, be willing to take a risk and invite someone to lunch or coffee. The benefits far outweigh the risks. I truly hate to imagine how much harder it would have been for Leigh if she and her family had to return Baby that day alone.

Amazingly, there is a happy ending to Leigh's story. She received a call from a lawyer over a year later asking her if she would still take Baby. His adoption was finalized prior to the final editing of this book.

The Same?

In our quest for equality, women seemed to be driven to be the *same*. Couldn't equal rights exist in respectful understanding of *differences*? Men went out and worked, so we think we should. Men earned lots of money, so we should as well. We've succeeded admirably. Now we have equal or better rates of heart attacks and stress. And no one is home with the kids.

We've made great strides in having our rights honored. Women are often enjoying fascinating careers and good incomes. With our welfare reform, we've even imposed the excitement of career-over-motherhood on our most vulnerable mother-baby pairs so that Mom can be assured a great job at McDonald's while her baby languishes in sub-standard day care.

One may wonder if we have not created a situation of enslavement, rather than freedom. Our dual-wage culture has created higher demands: more expensive gifts, higher level of participation in expensive events, additional expectations in appearance, and for those women who stay home, further isolation. Women are often not "choosing career," but rather forced to work just to stay afloat in an economy propelled by dual wages. She was not informed before being saddled with a huge mortgage just how much her heart would break when she said goodbye to her six-week-old baby upon return to her job.

Given the fact that we know that childbearing and breastfeeding are states of health that women are designed to experience, it would also follow that what we are promoting applies to high-risk as well as low-risk women. Adolescent mothers and older first-time mothers, rich women and poor women, healthy and sickly women would all benefit from rediscovery of the biological model and natural design. When we deviate from that, trouble ensues. Teen moms could be assisted to finish school while mothering babies. Mothers without financial resources would be ahead if they were not paying for formula after the federal assistance runs out. Mothers who are not optimally healthy would reap benefits adding to health by following the model. Relationships between less-skilled, less-educated mothers and their babies could not help but benefit from more solid attachments. Yet, these are precisely the women who are less likely to receive good teaching and support about their births and breastfeeding.

Perhaps, in the end, women have become disempowered and dethroned in the very arena which was once their reigning province.

Stone Age Babies and Techno Moms

By Nancy Williams

The solution to adult problems tomorrow depends (in) large measure upon how our children grow up today.

—Margaret Mead

What a mother does with her baby matters. Mothers shape their children in long-lasting and measurable ways, bestowing upon them some of the emotional attributes

they will possess and rely on, to their benefit or detriment, for the rest of their lives.

—Amini, Lannon, & Lewis, 2000

Civilization will commence on the day when the well-being of the new-born baby prevails over any other consideration.

—Wilhelm Reich

In all the so-called "Mommy Wars," from the 60s forward, the question of what might be good for the babies seldom is asked. The focus has been on what women want, especially in the realm of economic concerns. Oh, yes, there have been studies of school performance of children who grew up in day care. There have been those who have demonstrated that those daughters are more likely to achieve scholastically and to be successful career women themselves. Seldom do we find mention of the question of how old the child was when Mom returned to work. Once a child is older, separations are tolerated, but an infant/toddler is an entity unlike any other. All in all, we seem to be living with an unspoken presumption that children will be "OK" without Mom.

Is "OK" good enough? Is that the best we have to offer to our children?

Do we stop to ask how these changes might affect the mother-baby relationship? And does that matter? If so, what is the impact of these changes for the mother and baby?

With all there is at stake, even asking these questions is culturally painful. In the film *Awakenings*, the lead character, Dr. Sayer, is visiting with an elderly doctor who had treated encephalitis patients in previous decades. Dr. Sayer is suspicious that his newly acquired chronic patients may have much more going on in their experience than previously thought by hospital staff, who refer to them as "vegetables," assuming no cognitive or emotional life is present. The elderly doctor contends that the patients have lost cognition in their apparently vacant state. "Are you certain?" Dr. Sayer asks, followed by, "How do you know?" "Because the alternative is unthinkable," says the elder. He could not face the horror of an alternative theory allowing for "chronics" actually to be feeling, experiential beings, which did in fact reveal itself to be true.

Perhaps these questions of all things mother-baby related are hard to explore because of the potential indictment of our own choices and experience. Perhaps the knowledge of how we have potentially harmed our children becomes an "unthinkable alternative."

For a century now, ignorance sustained by denial and further walled off by defensiveness has prevented us from a true understanding of the needs of mothers and babies.

People are often vilified for simply raising the question. Yet, given the import, how can we continue to blissfully avoid it? Television and movies perpetuate the idea that babies do just fine and have good relationships with absent parents. How often have we seen a story line about a doctor who works ninety hours a week, frustrated because she will miss her daughter's soccer playoffs, yet lovingly connecting with her in the evening as if all is well? Because the *mother's* experience is that she loves her child more than life, the assumption is that even in her absence, the child also experiences the maternal love. Or we see the characters on the television show *Friends* who have a baby that seemingly never cries or demands care, except when there is opportunity for humor about breastmilk or nanny storylines. Not once do we see this single mother struggle with sleep deprivation, keeping her laundry folded, or any of the day-to-day difficulties of motherhood, particularly for those doing it solo.

The film *No Country for Old Men* begins with a prologue that puzzles over the changing severity of criminality, just in the lifetime of the retiring sheriff. The speaker tells of a time when the sheriff may have completed his career without ever carrying a gun. The remainder of the movie demonstrates not only the new need for him to have a gun and use forceful protection, but also a new level of violence coupled with lack of conscience which is not only more common, but more insidiously evil in its evidence.

Is there an answer to these questions of causation? What is known about the formation of the infant brain or the development of conscience and empathy? Actually, we know quite a bit.

A secure attachment developed and sustained during the first three years of life can be seen as equaling the "immune system" for trauma. Not only does the child learn better social referencing—that is, being able to determine the proper response in a new social encounter—but he also has more strength and resilience when an encounter results in pain. So, he is less likely to enter a negative situation since his internal red flags are waving, but if he does he is better equipped to resolve it.

Conscience and empathy develop in the context of a secure attachment. They form and develop in the arms of loving parents. As the baby experiences distress, his parents will rock him, nurse him, coo at him, walk him, and sing to him. This helps him to be calmed and at the same time learn how to calm himself as he "memorizes" what they do to help him. Over time, after many repeated episodes of loving comfort, he eventually learns how to regulate his own emotional state. He learns to calm his own anxiety or anger and to comfort his sadness. This is called "self-regulation" and is a precursor to empathy, conscience, and mental health. This process, well known to developmental scientists, flies in the face of some popular parenting books which tell parents that the baby will learn how to soothe himself if left to cry in the crib. His brain is not equipped to learn this on his own.

Actually if left alone in that way, what he will learn instead is that he should stop calling for help since no one will come. He will learn that it is a hard world and he is on his own, his brain actually wiring itself into a somewhat-permanent anxious state. Without the ability to self-regulate, when he becomes upset, he won't be able to moderate the intensity of his emotions and may react with violence, or other inappropriate responses. He will experience so many moments of anger that it becomes part of the fabric of his response. This mode of survival that he has learned is part of a self-absorption that precludes conscience and empathy. His ability to be resilient is also compromised. The rage he feels when screaming for help that never arrives becomes his default emotion.

This scenario makes it more difficult to successfully complete Erikson's (first) stage of "Trust versus Mistrust." He learns instead that there is no one to trust. His experience of trust can only occur when caretakers respond to his cries, teaching him that he can trust his ability to ask for help as well as trust in those around him to care for his needs. Less severe results may include the husband who reacts by hitting his wife as he hasn't learned a healthy response to stress. In common instances of parental non-responsiveness, as he grows he may look just a little self-absorbed. If this is a more intensely experienced stream of events for him as an infant, he might develop a personality disorder such as narcissism. If the lack of response is relentless enough, Bruce Perry and other trauma experts have evidence to suggest that he may never develop the capacity for empathy or love at all, perhaps becoming a sociopath.

An additional aspect to this is the wiring of implicit memory in the brain. The hippocampus stores these "emotional memories" as experiences that have no cognitive description for the preverbal child. The result is that the core of what we believe about relationships is formed here. One example would be that if the baby has a responsive parent, he will forever associate crying with comfort and connection, leading to the ability to feel safe and secure. If he has parents who are not well-connected to him, perhaps living by a book or schedule, his unanswered cries of distress leave associations with anger, fear, and rejection. Ultimately he sees relationships as painful things and approaches them with anxiety, functioning within them in a very unsatisfactory manner.

Another important question is one that seeks to understand where we are relationally. Are children growing up to be able to sustain marriages for the long term? What kind of partners do they choose?

How are their parenting skills—will they respond to their own babies or be paralyzed by the horror of their own unmet needs when the baby cries? This is one of the psychological dynamics that leads a mother—who truly loves her child—to respond to him in a negative, even abusive manner such as impatience, irritation or anger, Shaken Baby Syndrome, and the like.

What friendships can these children engage throughout their lives?

American culture values materialism and consumerism, in addition to rugged individualism. These often eclipse family, relationships, spirituality, and community. Perhaps we have taken this to an extreme as we seem to have lost sight of the fact that humans are hard-wired for relationship. Freshly emerged from the womb, the blinking baby will attempt to focus his eyes and seek a human face, responding to various facial expressions from the start. He eagerly tries to track sounds until he is able to connect them to a face. Every moment in a baby's life includes behaviors that seek human contact in the form of eye contact, touch, or sound. Even in sleep, a baby will move and gravitate closer to Mom's body if it is available.

We Americans are so obsessed with individualism that once a toddler is walking and talking we see him as autonomous, capable of adult behaviors. We practically hand a one-year-old a briefcase and tell him to start achieving. We have expectations of facility that is beyond his biologic abilities. We treat our children as "little adults" and expect them to behave as such.

Possibly our drive towards independence might better be reconfigured as a drive toward *interdependence*. We have much knowledge of the biological benefits of close relationship. One of many examples is that our blood pressure lowers when we are with a loving partner. Studies show that having even a dog or cat is far superior to being alone.

The Musketeers' famous slogan describes this interdependence beautifully, "One for all and all for one." Yes, the individual is important enough for the group to defend, yet the group is also what the individual will give his life to protect interdependence.

Recently a young man was describing the mindset of his friends and colleagues towards the needs of others. He said that for the most part, the youngest adult generation has an attitude of "How sad for you—not my problem." A deepening of self-interest above all else seems to be creeping into our society. One wonders how much of that may be due to a basic failure of the attachment system, then exacerbated by delayed marriage and childbearing, those seminal events that launch us into true adulthood. A generation ago, women married and began families in their early twenties, if not shortly after high school. Now the average age of first marriage for a woman is 28. Young adults are missing the experiences known to form self and identity in positive ways. Instead self and identity seem to be emerging in the context of Me Only.

As I transitioned between my various careers of mothering, perinatal consultant and educator, and finally Marriage and Family Therapist, I found myself fascinated and puzzled by what appears to me to be a major disconnect of what is known in the world of perinatal health and development versus what is known in medicine versus theories and research in psychology. While Attachment Theory is taught in any graduate course on human development, still the application of it to babies and families appears to be lacking. Many times I have witnessed conference speakers, authors, and teachers dodging questions and hedging when asked about whether mothers need to be with babies on a continual basis. When pressed, they acknowledge this truth and go on to describe the "attacks" they receive for such statements.

My clients often help to crystallize my thinking about these topics. Not too long ago the light bulb finally went on about what I believe may be another problem in the attachment realm. Much has been written and discussed about the rebellions of the sixties and decades to follow. Many things in our world changed around that time, not the least of which was that we were for the first time experiencing an entire generation of children who were bottle-fed and raised with the resultant reduced maternal attachment.

Perhaps one unforeseen result was an increase in "Irish Twins," i.e., siblings born very close together. Such a phenomenon does occur when exclusive breastfeeding is in place, but it is rare. The biology suggests that babies do best if they are born more than two years apart. Research has born this out: two years between pregnancies provides lower risk for maternal and infant problems, including risk reduction for SIDS. Additionally, a baby requires such intense parenting for at least the first two years that a new baby intrudes in a way that means the first one's needs will not be met. I have seen this as a regular occurrence in my clients: If they have a slightly younger sibling, they are more likely to have attachment problems.

Neurons that fire together, wire together. People who are able to attend to one another, touch, talk, and connect also fire together, wire together, and survive together.

—*Wisdom and the Adult Brain*, Author unknown

What do we know about the formation of human relationships? In the last fifty years, we have actually acquired a large amount of hard data relative to understanding the genesis of human interaction and connection. In addition to years of observation, study, and conclusions, we now have amazing technology such as Functional MRIs, PET scans, and the like, which allow us to actually observe the brain. We can watch it grow and develop before birth and throughout the rest of life. What was once a matter of educated conjecture has now been confirmed as hard data.

Moms and babies rely on their limbic (emotional) system to communicate, as baby is primarily right-brain dominant during the first three years of life. This limbic communication is generally pleasurable and builds an internal sense of a child's self by confirming feeling. Baby cries and Mom picks him up and coos at him. He laughs and her face lights up as she laughs with him. Relationship regulates normal neurophysiology, i.e. biochemical brain function. The mother's and baby's neurons actually fire in synchrony, creating a special intimacy.

It isn't long until Mother and Baby develop an emotional rhythm, based on their temperaments, personalities, and other factors. Babies *require* this synchronous continual interaction, which is known as limbic resonance. This creates a sensory window for each into the other's brain. This emotional harmonizing is a partial explanation for the phenomenon of dogs being able to sense an impending seizure in humans with whom they have a bond. We rely on the resultant limbic "intelligence" every day as we read social cues Babies who are separated regularly from mother cannot experience the same level of synchrony. Think of what a dance would be like with multiple partners cutting in every five steps. Many babies are trying to keep up with the dance while trading caregivers, which does not allow them to develop resonance with another individual. . Our ability to get "in sync" with others becomes particularly important when we are faced with dangerous people, as our emotional intelligence sends alarms from our limbic to cognitive brain. One problem that psychopaths have is that they don't receive input from limbic to cognitive systems of the brain.

Babies cry to tell us that something isn't right. They often start with a bit of fussing and continue to escalate their cries as they experience the greater distress of not being heard and responded to. They are actually very adept at communicating when things are awry if the caretakers give them the respect of listening and responding, learning each new little person's "cues" or individual language. The person with whom the baby has limbic resonance is most likely also the most skilled at knowing how to respond. Her consistent, loving reply to her baby's communication helps him to feel "righted" when his emotional or physical experience has caused discomfort. Both of them are chemically "happier" when this occurs.

What is the result of babies not being responded to? Not so long ago, it was believed that it was good for babies to cry—that it exercised their lungs and increased circulation, as well as showing them "who is boss."

As it turns out, this notion was wrong from every angle. When a baby cries for as little as ten minutes, several negative physiological consequences occur. His blood pressure increases, sometimes leading to minuscule brain bleeds. Oxygenation decreases, and he experiences detrimentally high releases of cortisol. A simple explanation is that it is as if this extra cortisol coats his brain in a toxic wash. Meanwhile, the developing connections in his brain are being wired for a state of anxiety, depression, or other mood problems which can last his lifetime if this is a regular occurrence. Additionally, his immature immune function will be compromised.

Where is the evidence that crying and separation are *not* harmful? The assumption exists in outdated professional opinion and popular parenting theory, yet there is no data supporting such assumptions; in fact quite the opposite has been shown. Yet we continue to laugh at babies while they cry, ignore them, stuff a pacifier in their mouth, or worse.

There is a dramatic difference between a baby's physiological experience of crying alone in a crib versus that of crying in the arms of a loving parent who is dancing around the room with him, singing songs of comfort. Which would you prefer if you were struggling with a stomach ache, sadness, or fear? Often, those adults who prefer to suffer alone are themselves the victims of attachment disorders.

What about the concern of "spoiling" this baby by constantly picking him up? Training books are often popular largely because of their appeal to our selfishness in combination with the promises of all things great in parenting, such as a long night of sleep and a "good" child. These books are full of warnings to let the baby cry until it is "time" to eat, or until the parent has a whim to hold him, so as not to create bad habits of dependency. Such writings are in direct opposition to a very large body of evidence to the contrary. Ideas about a baby "manipulating" his parents are simply in error. The ability to manipulate requires cognitive abilities that don't yet exist in infancy. Babies are emotionally mature, but not cognitively so. Current knowledge of this is the exact opposite of what was thought for quite some time.

When it comes to parenting you can "do the time" when they are little or you can "do the time" when they are big. Although it is true that babies who are left to cry will eventually stop (making parenting easier and allowing parents to sleep), the other truth is that they will do this at a high cost to the foundations of their relationship to Mom and Dad, as well as the foundations of their mental and relational health. Trying to institute parenting shortcuts when they are small will likely only result in much more disconcerting problems during their adolescence. Parents may slumber peacefully through infancy only to be deprived of many nights sleep fifteen years later while awaiting a troubled daughter's return home late at night or not at all.

Much has been studied about trauma and its impact on child development. The baby's experience of separation and "crying it out" is not culturally defined as traumatic because it is so commonplace. However, when Mom is either absent or otherwise unavailable to him (unresponsive or intrusive), his biological and psychological template interprets this as trauma. The fact that it is now common does not dilute his experience of terror, anxiety, grief, and the like. Additionally, should this child experience another major trauma during childhood, given that the brain was not wired for resilience, the trauma will be that much more damaging.

Pediatric neurologist Harry Chugani, who studies early brain development, notes, "There is no doubt that experience molds the young brain. The early years determine how the brain turns out" (Schore, 2001). He goes on to make clear that the child's potential is determined in the early years—from the first moment of life to countless hours spent in day care. He says, "These are the years when we create the promise of a child's future. This is when we set the mold" (Schore, 2001). Many scientists have said that kindergarten is not the starting point of the child's brain development. They say that by kindergarten the process is half over (Schore, 2001).

Do all babies' brains develop the same way, assuming good health and nutrition? In a word: no.

By eighteen weeks of gestation, the vast majority of the neurons are already formed, to the tune of 100 billion. Then the connections (synapses) must form so that the neurons can "talk" to each other in the form of chemical releases (neurotransmitters). This will occur at the rate of approximately 18 million connections per second in the growing brain. The number of synapses doubled twice during gestation, and will double again from birth to eight months.

During this time there is also the possibility to develop abnormalities in neurotransmission: too much or too little dopamine, seratonin, or norepinepherine systems, to name a few. One end result is that the stress response system is modulated incorrectly. In simple terms, the "wrong" chemicals are released in the brain at the "wrong" times, which can cause things such as depression and anxiety etc.

Proper development, then, is dependent on the environment. In other words, these connections will form in a way that is conducive to sound mental health—or not. The improper formation could easily lead to problems such as mood disorders, particularly when there is genetic predisposition.

Anthropologist Meredith Small reports another possible problem when attachment doesn't occur to form a healthy brain. In her article "What you Can Learn from Drunk Monkeys" (July, 2002), she describes monkeys who are allowed to bond normally to their mothers and colonies, as well as those who were separated from mothers. Alcohol was offered in the cages of both groups. While most of the monkeys from both tasted it, only those who had been denied a healthy mother-baby relationship developed alcoholism. Once again, if a genetic predisposition is in place, insecure or disorganized attachment may prompt the expression of the gene that predisposes the individual to alcoholism.

My grandfather was a prime example. Our family is made up in part of ethnicities known to have a propensity for alcoholism. Unfortunately his mother didn't particularly want him, especially since he was a boy. Her displeasure showed during his growing up, never allowing him to bond with her. He began years of serious drinking when he was an adolescent.

My grandfather's story, presented as a study of one, is a demonstration of how lack of attachment is one of several potential causes of addiction or other problems in adult life. It would be a mistake to suggest that every difficulty is caused by attachment. Yet, a healthy attachment has such a significant impact on the development of a young child's brain that often this is but the first step to disorders. If the child then experiences other trauma or major relational problems as they grow, there may come a perfect developmental storm that results in an addiction, mental disorder, personality, or relational disorders.

The limbic system is much more mature at birth than are the cognitive structures. This results in the infant experiencing many emotional events, which are stored in his memory as part of his template for relationships. Later, this template affects who he is attracted to and how he gets along with others, as well as his ability to sustain lifelong relationships. Advertisers are very knowledgeable about this phenomenon and use it to sell their products, hoping to create an attachment between the consumer and their brand.

One of many areas to be formed in the first months is the orbitofrontal area of the brain. This is the region where ultimately the child will have judgment, impulse control, and ability to predict consequences. When this does not take shape properly, not only might you see a preschooler with problems, but also as an adolescent he will be behind the curve in his decision-making abilities.

The process of completion of this important area of cognitive function is facilitated in part by secure attachment. It's not enough to protect a child from trauma, though it certainly is a basic requirement. Optimal development also requires love and nurturing. Bonding and attachment can only occur when two people are physically near each other, engaging in frequent touch. This promotes a sharing of neuronic activity in both brains.

When I was raising small children, I ran an in-home daycare. I could barely stand to watch my little charges endure the separation from their love objects. When their mothers left, babies who had recently begun daycare would often scream in protest for hours each day before they gave up and settled into the predicted state of despair, emotionally withdrawn, lethargic, and refusing my repeated offers of nurturing. I have vivid memories burned into my brain of these poor little people in heaps, on their "blankies" by the front door, refusing to be comforted or distracted. Did they eventually adjust? Yes....but I've always wondered about the emotional cost of what was obviously a very traumatic event for them.

By the time their mothers returned each day, they had often pulled themselves together. I tried to broach the subject with the mothers a few times and was virtually always met with strong resistance. Eventually these children and I would bond, only to have to be separated as they grew older and went to school, or occasionally because, as the mother said, "I can't stand how he loves you." While this definitely hurt my heart, I can only imagine the damage done to these children with all of these broken attachments in such a short lifetime. I have adult coping skills while the little guys don't. I've had students who talked about having twelve nannies in their first two years of life. How can a little person form a secure attachment in such circumstances?

When lovers break up, a large part of the pain is that the brain and body have an expectation of the presence of the loved one. If s/he is gone, the brain releases chemicals of sorrow. Why would we expect it to be different when a baby is missing his love, to whom he is addicted?

Two other incidents were important in developing my interest in attachment. My husband and I were foster parents of Todd from the time he was one until three and suffered the pain of the broken attachment. The day he was to leave our home, we sat with him, trying to explain the unexplainable, only to have him beg through his tears to let him try to "be a good boy so I can stay." He had no ability to understand court orders. All he knew was that his love objects and family were going away. Over 25 years later, my adult heart still longs to be with him and occasionally in my dreams I envision him running into my arms. He has probably forgotten us on a cognitive level, but his "emotional memory" of loss has likely been the source of many problems. Worse, this loss was on top of the loss of his biological mother to liquor when he was a baby.

The final event in developing my interest in attachment was the challenge made to me personally by the author of some parenting-by-schedule books to disprove his theses. This popular author with no training in medicine, social science, psychology or child development makes claims that his "method" guarantees a healthy outcome. Evidence to the contrary caused me great alarm. I began to search for whatever I could find in print and of course engaged in serious observation of people around me.

So it was with great interest that I discovered the research on bonding and attachment. Dr. John Bowlby actually stumbled upon his life's work, developing what would come to be called "Attachment Theory" as a result of coincidental observations of children in hospital where he was attending. He noted that young children, separated by hospitalizations, could be observed moving through the grief process, much like adults who have experienced the death of a loved on. Out of this work and in concert with Elisabeth Kubler-Ross, the model for the progression of grieving was developed.

In addition to watching these children grieve, he noted that their personalities changed permanently. Outgoing children would sometimes become withdrawn, while quiet compliant children might develop anxiety and acting-out behaviors after separations.

His student Mary Ainsworth was interested in exploring this further. Some of her work was done in an indigenous culture. She added a crucial piece to the research when she noted that it isn't enough for mother and baby to be in constant close proximity, but the mother needed to respond to the cues of the baby. It was the baby that elicited behaviors, not vice versa. If a mother was intrusive, trying to set feeding or play times, it proved to be detrimental to the fragile, still-developing bond. On the flip side, if the baby failed to elicit desirable responses from the mother, insecure attachment would be the likely outcome. Her work showed that babies need to lead the dance, not parents.

Such knowledge is in conflict with our current ideas on "quality time." How can one schedule their emotional needs? While it may be unarguable that children need the engagement with parents that theoretically comes with quality time, the reality is that children need large quantities of parental time *and* they need quality. Recently a popular comedian reported that he asked his kids if they preferred one day at Disneyland with him or every night at home. It is no surprise that they wanted him every night.

Ainsworth also conducted what she termed the Strange Experiment, where she studied twelve-month old babies with their mothers. A stranger was introduced into the room, the mother left, and in a short time she returned. Ainsworth was able to note distinctly different responses of these toddlers as they interacted with mothers and strangers, and as they reunited with the mothers who returned. She identified distinctly different "attachment styles" of secure, insecure anxious, and insecure avoidant, which she eventually demonstrated became *lifelong relational patterns*, set at a young age.

The goal of healthy adult relationship is to be separate but connected. By separate, we mean that one has a strong sense of self and comfort with who they are. One "owns" his/her thoughts, feelings, dreams, goals, and values, after having adopted them as their own, separately from the family of origin. By connected, we mean that one is able to share this "self" with another "self" and to enjoy intimacy—the warmth of being able to share those feelings, values, dreams. The ultimate expressions of this are lifelong close marriage, parenting, and relationships with adult (grown) children. This is not to be confused with those who have intense but short-lived relationships, as we often see in our attachment-disordered society. In fact it is just the opposite. Isn't it interesting that Baby Boomers, the first generation in recent history to experience hospital births to drugged mothers, bottle-feeding, and a detached style of parenting have themselves experienced astronomical divorce rates and difficulties with all manner of relationships? The generations to follow have only continued to fare worse.

As I teach college students these concepts, some have difficulty grasping the idea of long-term relationships. They ask, "I have a lot of hot weekends—does that mean I'm securely attached?" "I love my cat—is that what you mean?" No, this is about human relationships that are supportive in our lives for decades.

Erik Erikson's work analyzed psychological tasks to be completed at various ages and stages. He described the process of psychological tasks driven by crisis and healthy resolution. His work dovetails nicely with the observations of Ainsworth, who noted the importance of mother's responding to baby cues. His first stage is Trust versus Mistrust. The psychological crisis in infancy is to determine whether the baby's world is one in which he can trust others. When left to cry in a crib as a regular state of events, he learns that, try as he might, he cannot effect change or get his own needs met. He has to find a way to survive alone until he can get crumbs of attention from someone. Conversely, when a loving parent consistently picks him up, comforts him, feeds, and plays with him, he learns that this world is OK and he can trust the people around him. This first-year experience forms a template upon which to build the schemas of relationship as he develops. The emotional pattern of trusting and interdependence with others—or not—will determine the cut of the cloth of the rest of life's relationships.

Margaret Mahler, child psychoanalyst and co-author of *The Psychological Birth of the Human Infant: Symbiosis and Individuation*, written in 1975, added to these discussions by describing the stages of attachment she had observed in the first years of life, concluding that a disruption in these processes may result in a disturbance in one's ability to maintain a reliable sense of individual identity in adulthood.

In the first phase, named Symbiotic, Baby sees himself as one with mother, the two of them separated from the rest of the world. During symbiosis the baby "hatches," differentiating self from mother, and becomes interested in the world. The next phase is Separation, marked first by "practicing." During this time, (nine to sixteen months), baby still feels at one with Mother but begins moving away as he explores the world through his new locomotion abilities.

As he moves into his toddlerhood he must resolve the fears and crisis of Autonomy. He will move back and forth between needing Mother constantly to, "No! Do it self!" all the while using her as what Ainsworth referred to as a Secure Base in order to do this experimenting. A nursing toddler will often run to Mother, nurse a few seconds in order to release milk and then run off even as the milk sprays in his wake. Unfortunately for American babies, this time of newly developing independence is often misunderstood and the mother may misread this need and respond with impatience or unavailability. Should she continue to offer herself in a nurturing, responsive way, the child emerges from this process with a strong, healthy sense of self and ability to enjoy others.

These theories were born from studies of families who were the norm at the time, mother at home and sometime engaging in long-term breastfeeding. Margaret Mahler's work, adding to what Ainsworth had noted, looked specifically at babies' interactions with a constantly available (nursing) mother. She found that development unfolded optimally in the constant presence of the mother through the first years.

In recent years, many other scientists have built on the work of the early researchers, such as Robert Karen, Allan Schore, Thomas Lewis, and Bruce Perry. Early theory has been validated time and again. It is a sad commentary that political obstacles often restrain both research and reporting of results.

Decades of working with families has left no doubt in our minds that babies know what they are doing. They are equipped with abilities to have their needs met by signaling parents. Crying is of course the most obvious way they have of asking for help, but it is only the most desperate of means that the baby has. Baby drives the attachment process, arriving with the ability to elicit loving response from his parents. He does this by smelling sweet, by engaging in eye contact and turning towards us, by self-latching to a breast, and by snuggling into our necks and bodies. While he does not have the cognitive ability to manipulate us as was once thought, he has a rather complete ability to engage us in relationship if we are healthy enough to pay attention. When parents respond they come to know and understand who this little person is. Later, as the baby does garner new mental ability, parents are more effective with gently disciplining him and telling him that he can't have candy right before dinner. The child has taught them what he needs. And so it is that attentive parents will also know from the relationship when he is ready for separations, more emotional challenges, and so forth. The child will also wean when he is ready, though that may be later than the parents have been conditioned to expect.

Attachment and healthy independence are not opposites, but rather cause and effect. Secure, loving attachments between parent and child lead to strong independence and healthy interdependence. This is what the data shows to be true as the attachment continues throughout the parenting relationship, even during adolescence. As the child moves into adulthood, the attachment evolves into lifelong friendship between the parents and adult child.

The truth is quite opposite of the notion behind frequent phone calls from concerned mothers. "I'm worried that I've spoiled my baby. She just wants to be held (be with me, see me,) all the time. That can't be good."

Yes, it can and it is. Do we want our children to learn to seek comfort and enjoyment from loving people or from plastic pieces or other artificial objects of "love"? When we became foster parents of a toddler, it was heartbreaking to watch him sing to, stroke, and hug and kiss his bottle, giving his affection to an inanimate object that was unable to love him back. It should have been his mother who was receiving such joyous affection, responding in kind.

In a poem written from the perspective of one lover to another, we might also hear the healthy attachment of a mother to her child of any age.

i carry your heart with me (i carry it in
my heart)i am never without it(anywhere
i go you go, my dear; and whatever is done
by only me is your doing, my darling

—ee cummings, "I Carry Your Heart With Me"

REPLACING THE IRREPLACEABLE MOTHER

BY NANCY WILLIAMS

If this is all about relationship, then one has to question the assumption that all is well as long as diapers are changed, stomachs filled, and brains stimulated. Certainly those are basic needs which cannot be ignored. But the fact is that *no one* will love Baby as much as his parents, with the possible exception of extended family members who also have a long-term investment in this child. The best "sitters" in the world by definition cannot engage in the attachment needed by the baby. If the baby spends so much time with the caretaker as to somehow form a secure attachment, the temporary nature of the caretaker's role means that there will be an attachment wound which may be significant and may come at a very vulnerable time in the young child's life. When mother changes daycare providers or little Johnny goes to preschool when he is two or three years old, his object of attachment (his first daycare provider) is "dead" to him. He grieves just as surely as I would if my best friend had died, though he doesn't have the maturity and skills to move through the process in a way that doesn't leave damage.

Secure attachment empowers the mother to know how to effectively care for and interact with her baby, teaching her to be a good mother. Further, it develops neural networks in the baby's brain, most specifically on the right hemisphere and in the frontal lobe —crucial to healthy emotional function.

Despite all of this research and work, the prevailing notions on childrearing in Western cultures still seem to revolve around behaviorism, the theoretical constructs that Harlow et al were able to disprove. Helping parents to learn to "extinguish" the "undesirable" behavior of crying in infants is the direct teaching of B. F. Skinner, who used it to train behaviors of rodents in his famous rat boxes through "operant conditioning." The irony is that we know that babies who are responded to in a nurturing, prompt manner cry less than those whose behaviors are shaped through rewards and punishments as the Skinner rats were.

Changing the national outlook on mothers and babies is difficult because our culture seems to accept, whether spoken or not, that our babies will be fine and will develop well as long as their basic physical needs are met. At a recent court hearing regarding a custody dispute, the judge questioned expert testimony on attachment by pointing to his clerk and asking if she is putting her baby at risk by coming back to work. The question was asked with a bit of sarcasm implying an unwillingness to hear the answer, placing the expert witness in a difficult position. On another occasion, a participant in hearings regarding local welfare programs raised the question about bonding and attachment for the mothers and babies in this at-risk population. She was roundly criticized and told that one author of the new program was a congressperson who was also a new mother. She was going back to work, so why couldn't these mothers who were on welfare? Perhaps the congressperson had the resources for live-in help or a nanny to accompany her to the office, which would mean less time of separation from her baby. Mothers receiving welfare will not have any such resources. Further, is it a wise choice simply because a congresswoman has made it?

Studies have shown that children who were in day care do well later on—they make good grades in school and demonstrate independence and self-sufficiency. Many of these studies compared children in programs such as Head Start or other government-run day care situations. Possibly, these mothers have enough painful distraction in their lives that they are functionally unable to provide for their children and this group does achieve more after being in such programs than they might if left solely in the dysfunctional home.

Who, though is looking at how they form relational competence? Is academic success our most important measure of proficiency in life? Who is taking the long view, asking what deficits might become apparent during adolescence and into adulthood?

Consider the difference in experience between two babies. One is with his mother almost all of the time. Scores of times during the day he looks into her eyes and, just as with adult lovers, he sees happiness and joy reflected there, causing him to feel important and loved. His friend is in daycare 35 hours a week. The provider loves children and does her best to engage. But she is not "addicted" to this baby. She is not in love with him. She also has other children to take care of and so his time of seeing loving reflection in her eyes is severely limited compared with his friend. What differences will result not only in how their brains form and function but also in their relationships over their lifetimes?

Tipping Point

So we have come to this, with common experiences in our lives: breast cancer, personality and mood disorders, crime, divorce, higher perinatal mortality, infertility, unexpected teen pregnancy. Young adults are afraid to marry and start families, delaying their own maturation. A generation is so poorly socialized that we no longer have boundaries of politeness and appropriate speech and behavior. We now have new rights as women, paid for by the loss of our ability to enjoy those few brief years of being with our young children. A typical baby is spending his days grieving the loss of the mother who is at work fighting for a place to pump her swelling breasts and cry for the baby who is away from her.

Is this really what any of us want? Shall we ask the babies to vote?

We've left the biological model and now have to replace it with gimmicks, programs, and all manner of substitutes (i.e. bottles, pacifiers, blankies and teddy bears).

Connecting the Dots

Not long ago, I once again watched a mother-baby dyad as they gazed into each other's eyes, clearly in love. Madly, deeply in love, no less than an adult couple who have been together for just a few months. Perhaps mother replacements make as much sense as having someone stand in as our spouse or partner. Next time your spouse mentions an out of town business trip, ask if he minds if you find another man to keep you company while he is gone. Of course, the idea of this is ludicrous. Why then do we accept the same for our infants? When we are in love, do we derive the same satisfaction from having dinner with a substitute as we would with our lover? Isn't that the actual heart of the betrayal of adultery? If the unique relationship between two people itself is the key, we can't then expect that substitutes are, by definition, even possible.

Our culture has developed a long list of mother substitutes. We replace a mother's breast with pacifiers and other rubber nipples, her milk with formula, the warmth of her body with an isolette and machines to provide substitute temperature regulation, respiratory stimuli and cardiac function. We surrender her soft arms to car seats and strollers. We ask the youngest children to fend for themselves in a way that adults don't even manage. One woman recently said that she doesn't sleep well when her husband is away, musing on what it would be like to be a small child alone in a big, cold room. While adults seldom wish to sleep alone, we've exchanged nighttime connection for cribs and other solitary confinement.

"I don't want to be a human pacifier!" "You are just letting the baby use you as a pacifier." These oft-repeated, disdainful remarks ignore the fact that being a "human pacifier" is exactly what we are *designed* to do. It is the little plastic thing that is an aberration. "He wants to be held all the time and wakes up the minute I put him down." Again, the abnormal state is one of separation, not one of togetherness.

Mothers and babies share intimacy that is unparalleled in any other relationship. The closest thing would be the couple who have just fallen in love, but even it doesn't have the inherent biological connection of a mother and her baby. The adults "can't live" without each other, can't keep their hands off of each other, and grieve to the point of anorexia and insomnia when absence intrudes into their joy. Could it be possible that one culprit in the causes of postpartum depression is simply the mother's distress at having to leave her love object, and the repressed feeling that she "can't live" without him?

With all the changes in expectation, we don't even know what normal is anymore. Toddlers who wake up several times are the norm within circles where they are still breastfeeding and the parents have found ways to deal with this and still get adequate sleep themselves, yet these children are defined as "disordered" by sleep experts. It's too bad that the mothers of centuries gone by are not available to use as scientific "controls" or wise advisors.

The biology of the mother-baby relationship and its symbiotic quality is exquisite.

It's all about relationship! How can the love object be replaced? Do we replace an absent husband or wife for an overnight companion or for eight hours each day and feel secure and content as adults? No, and neither can our babies. How can we expect Mom or Baby to be happy when they are grieving separation and violating their biology and heart's desire? Perhaps a problem with the Mommy Wars is the insistent focus on careers and the maternal pursuit of happiness to the exclusion of the needs of babies. There's an assumption that if someone fed, changed, and cuddled the baby, that was all that was required. After all, he wouldn't remember his infancy anyway. His brain was so immature that it couldn't be registering anything in a meaningful way, we thought. So, if Mommy went to work and had "quality day care" for her baby, it was thought to be just fine.

An unintended maternal consequence of abdicating her biologically designed role is often grief. She may wake up one morning realizing that she has missed her child's babyhood. Or that the childhood flew by while she was in business meetings or teaching other people's children. No matter how worthy her work is, she misses out on the relationship as well as the baby himself. But she has better coping skills than Baby does, and other support. She can look at his pictures or nanny cam. She can smell his little t-shirt and look forward to reuniting with him, knowing the separation is temporary. Still she grieves. For him, the separation is horrific in its seeming finality. All he knows is that his love object is nowhere to be seen with no hope of return because he hasn't yet developed "object permanence," the understanding that an unseen object may still exist elsewhere.

In talking about parenting her three children, Anna Quindlen writes:

> *But the biggest mistake I made is the one that most of us make while doing this. I did not live in the moment enough. This is particularly clear now that the moment is gone, captured only in photographs. There is one picture of the three of them sitting in the grass on a quilt in the shadow of the swing set on a summer day, ages 6, 4, and 1. And I wish I could remember what we ate, and what we talked about, and how they sounded, and how they looked when they slept that night. I wish I had not been in such a hurry to get on to the next thing: dinner, bath, book, bed. I wish I had treasured the doing a little more and the getting it done a little less.* —Anna Quindlen

Somewhere along the way, we forgot to question how we would meet the emotional needs of the baby. Given the fact that a child needing early medical or psychological intervention and care can cost taxpayers in excess of $1 million, we need to look at this simply from a practical point of view. Dr. Bruce Perry stated in a workshop that we have the richest society in terms of culture, possessions, and such and yet we are experiencing our own de-evolution by the way we are taking care of young children.

Perhaps our de-evolution has left us all on crutches, hobbling along and longing for something more fulfilling.

At many points in history, views of children have been rather negative, with younger children and babies bearing the brunt of the negativity. Until the 1980's it was common to do surgeries on babies without anesthesia, assuming that there wasn't much going on that would allow them to feel pain. One mother, grieving her baby's death, uncovered the truth of his surgery and became convinced that he died, in part, in response to his pain. She went on a campaign and changed the course of pediatric medicine and the use of anesthesia. Along the same lines, parents of the 50's were taught that babies were emotionally vacant, though cognitively sophisticated enough to "manipulate" their parents and to commit other evil acts.

Bowlby and his followers were able to demonstrate that the opposite is true. While cognition is largely undeveloped in infancy, new brain-imaging shows us that the limbic system (the seat of emotion in the brain) is comparatively well-developed. There is a wealth of video documentation that babies cry in protest and then shut down in despair when separated from their mothers right from the moment of birth.

In questioning why today's women seemingly do not grasp the happiness once promised to them by feminism, Danielle Crittenden writes:

> ***They are the female partners at law firms who thought they'd made provisions for everything about their career—except for the sudden, unsuspected moment when they find their insides shredding the first day they return from maternity leave, having placed their infants in a stranger's arms. They are the young mothers who quit their jobs to be with their babies and who now feel anxiety and even a mild sense of embarrassment about what they have chosen to do—who look over their fences at the quiet backyards of two-career couples, wondering if they haven't done a foolish thing, and feeling a kind of isolation their mothers never knew. Above all, these women are the majority of us, women who are hoping to do everything—work, children, marriage—only to ask ourselves why the pieces haven't added up the way we'd like or why we are collapsing under the strain of it all and doing everything so badly.***

—*What our Mothers Didn't Tell Us*", p. 21 Simon & Schuster, NY, 1999

So now it seems that women have new pressure to add mothering to their ever-lengthening list of obligations. Notice that it is an add-on. We can't let it "define" us, nor can we allow ourselves to turn into "boring housewives." So instead, we want to work 8–6, with one-hour commutes each way, stop for groceries, cook a nice meal, be great lovers, all the while responding to a baby who needs to nurse about twelve times in a 24-hour period and wakes us several times a night. Is it any wonder that a vulnerable new mother finds herself so sleep deprived that she slips into mania, depression, and other maladies? Should we be surprised that in a culture that has accepted artificial mothering, with all of these obligations pressing her she decides to give up breastfeeding early? Perhaps it might be better if she could "add on" her career, after her children are less in need of her. Our last chapter will address the idea of "sequencing" as a means of accomplishing all of our goals in a less frenetic, painful fashion.

Wouldn't true feminism, instead of ignoring the biology that clearly shows differences between men and women, better serve women by educating and empowering them to use their unique intuition, hormonal makeup, and hearts' desires in order to wholeheartedly embrace mothering if they choose to be mothers? Wouldn't it promote the rights and responsibilities of motherhood?

Many writings focus on the difficulties with career: if you leave your career to mother, how do you restore your place, sharpen your knowledge and skills, and acquire financial parity? Few articles ask the other important question: if we are unable to create desired relationships with our children as they are small, how can that ever be repaired? How can we assist our children in repairing those broken bonds? Perhaps, rather than dogged determination to focus efforts on the uphill struggle towards these things at the expense of motherhood, our labors could be better utilized by creating strategies for reentry or even re-creation of career. We, the authors and our friends, had no trouble with career development when our children matured and needed us less. Raising children provides women with opportunities to build a wealth of skills that are valuable in the workplace. Often we have even found ourselves at an advantage, having developed instincts about people and abilities that we learned while nursing children. We have many decades to work for pay but only a few short years to enjoy our young children.

With all the emphasis on the mother and baby, how do the father, grandparents and other important people develop relationship with this new person? Often this concern drives new parents to insist that Mom pump her breasts or bottle-feed, so that Dad can share in the feeding. Perhaps this points to our innate understanding that bonding is accomplished through the processes inherent in feeding: eye-to-eye contact, touch, focused attention. The question begs to be asked as to whether the baby is biologically capable of forming multiple attachments in the early months. Seemingly, the research is saying "No." Further, any substitute "feeding" is just that—a substitute for mother and the design given by biology. Mother substitutes are always going to be inadequate.

All of this is not only less than optimal, but also unnecessary. New evidence shows that a father experiences his own biochemical changes as a result of Baby's arrival. When he holds *his* baby, his testosterone levels drop in favor of rising estrogens. He is programmed to bond with Baby. A grandmother who once breastfed has similar processes, as her prolactin and oxytocin levels will rise as she cradles her new grandbaby. Margie Deutsch Lash recounts her years as a teacher, sharing stories with her young students and experiencing powerful sensations of oxytocin release, much the same as she experienced while nursing her babies.

Not only does full immersion into motherhood give us the chemical support, skills, interest, and ability to raise children, but these contributions to our new-found "self" become part of who we are for life. Women who have raised young children develop skills and abilities that serve them when they re-enter the job force and as they interview. If they breastfed, their chemical reactions to relationships are positively altered, with some data suggesting that they enjoy "mothering" chemical releases while holding grandchildren or even the children that they may be caring for in their professions.

Skill sets learned by mothers at home can be used later, upon re-entry into career, for instance. Self-maturation that is promoted through the experience of motherhood, is used later, even in non-related work. While many examples could be given, let's look at the example of a professional negotiator. She is adept at hearing both sides and being able to sort through the entanglements of the disagreement. This is a skill that she learned as she helped a five-year-old learn to give up his time on the video game so that his little brother could have a turn. When I studied for my later-in-life career as a therapist, many of my life experiences were brought into play as I sought to understand the material. Taking my licensure exams, I found that the skills I had learned as a volunteer mother prepared me to excel easily. Friends who have gone on to be professional teachers, nurses, business managers, and others have all described the benefits of the life experiences inherent in mothering.

In 1997, I had the privilege of caring for a woman while she died. Catherine was elderly and in the end stage of cancer. Having outlived her family, we, her friends, stood between her and aloneness in this world. When she was taken to the hospital, I found myself relying on information that I had learned as a mother in order to assess her less-than-tangible needs. Though she was no longer speaking, I was able to make emotional contact with her in the same ways I did when my children were infants, relying on my gut, eye-to-eye contact and other visual cues, and touch. As it became clear that she was most uncomfortable (in pain) with hospital protocol, I used the advocacy skills I had developed while raising children and dealing with establishments and institutions. I took her to our home, as it was clear that she would be more comfortable. As her last night ensued, I was able to follow her cues in keeping her comfortable and saw her through a gentle release. How grateful I was to have such mothering experiences as training to deal with the end of life!

With all of these changes impacting us at our most vulnerable time--infancy—where has our society landed? What is it that we value? What practices support that value and would we keep? Where must we make course adjustments?

We Americans value egalitarianism and autonomy, that is we want things to be equal and we want our independence. Most of us see these as very good things. Yet, even these good things when taken to extremes can be harmful. Might we be in danger from such extremes with our new technologies and loss of interdependence to other human beings? Perhaps interdependence is the necessary context for our values to thrive.

In 1956, a group of American missionaries were killed when they attempted to reach out to a hidden people group, the Waodanis. The reason they wanted to help this group was that it was literally killing off one another. They so exalted the concepts of egalitarianism and autonomy that they literally had no concept of the group good or of setting aside one's own desires to help others. And so they began spearing friends, families, and enemies alike. By the early 50's, the death rate of the adults was 60% by spearing. It was predicted that their extinction was just a few years away. As explained by anthropologists Clayton and Carol Robarchek, this might serve as a cautionary tale for us should we lose sight of the value of interpersonal dependence in favor of autonomy. Today the Waodonis still live their lives in much the same way as they have for centuries, except that their notions of strict independence have been replaced with a new value of interdependence, and they now live in community with one another.

Physical prowess was not something I was taught to seek. Both my mother and grandmother put limitations on their bodies. (Or was it done for them) Hell, when they gave birth they were thoroughly drugged, such meager faith did doctors place in the workings of their bodies. Imagine, they were denied the one really glorious moment when a woman's' body can truly shine. It's no wonder my forbearers gave me so little support for my own physical being.

—Joan Anderson, *A Year by the Sea: Thoughts of an Unfinished Woman*, p 85-86, (1999)

WHAT HAPPENS TO THE STONE-AGED BABY IN THE HOSPITAL

BY GRETCHEN ANDREWS

Once upon a time women believed they could bring a child into the world without the aid of pharmaceuticals that altered their experience. Once upon a time women knew that the work of labor would culminate with the joy of bringing a baby into the world. Somewhere along the way women seem to have given away their power and bought into the idea that childbirth was terrifying and horrifically painful – an experience to dread and mute as much as possible. In the past century or so childbearing made a sharp turn down a path that is so different from other mammals that it hardly seems close to the birth experience human babies are hard-wired to expect.

Arriving at the Hospital

In a typical US hospital, more likely than not, a baby's birth is going to involve multiple interventions. As the mother-to-be walks in through the hospital doors, signs papers and dons the somewhat undignified gown stating, "Property of the XYZ Hospital," she experiences a metamorphosis from a healthy woman about to experience the most profound event of her life to a "patient," trading power and ownership for vulnerability and dependence. Her choices have just become drastically limited, as the hospital and its staff contend with legal liabilities and profit margins in an expensive and litigious society, with frequently overworked and underpaid staff.

Cultural expectations have a significant impact on the way a woman expects childbirth to be. If her experience of childbirth is limited to docudramas of all the things that can go wrong, or horror stories of the experiences of others, she is not likely to enter into her labor with positive expectations. By contrast, a young girl who has been present since an early age as a witness to the miracle of birth, and heard stories of mothers being surrounded by those who support and encourage their ability to birth their children, will go into her own experience with few fears and a much greater confidence in her body to perform the job of bringing her baby into the world without the need for multiple interventions.

Fear is a force that impedes confidence and can bring about choices that may not be in the mother's or the baby's best interests either for birth or afterward. A woman who has brought her child into the world without medication has experienced an incredible feat of endurance and strength. She is confident that her body has served her well and she brings that sense of "can do" into her mothering experience. In observing mothers who have not had this confidence-building experience, there seems to be a greater sense of doubt as to what they can do if there are feeding problems with their child after birth. Many who work intimately with the breastfeeding dyad note that mothers who give birth without pain medication generally have more tenacity to persist through any problems with feeding issues than do mothers who have not had that same empowering experience.

Effects of Pharmacology

Even before pharmaceuticals are introduced for pain management, a mother may receive medications that may have a negative impact on her birth experience. If she arrives at the hospital in labor and does not progress quickly enough in the eyes of the staff, or if she is past her due date, her health care provider may order an induction to help stimulate the onset of labor. When labor begins on its own, the pace of her contractions is generally within the mother's ability to handle. When labor is either induced or augmented with drugs, the strength of contractions caused by the artificial oxytocin (Pitocin) may make the intensity of her contractions too much to bear. While induction of labor is indicated under certain medical circumstances, it is often offered for reasons having nothing to do with medical issues that would validate its use such as preeclampsia, (persistent, severe high blood pressure, headaches, protein in the urine, and edema of the lower extremities) or if the pregnancy is more than two weeks overdue *and* there are definite signs of fetal distress. Far too often elective inductions (as opposed to medically indicated ones) happen before weekends or holidays and are timed so that the baby is delivered before dinnertime - at least the doctor's. (Wagner, 2006*)* The use of Pitocin via an intravenous (IV) drip is frequently a standard protocol for laboring women, even when labor is progressing well. This artificial ratcheting up of the intensity of labor can create fetal distress, making other interventions like episiotomy and vacuum extraction necessary to speed up the process of the delivery. None of these may have been necessary if labor had been allowed to run its normal course.

> Marsden Wagner, M.D., M.S. says:
>
> *Obstetricians "attend" 90 percent of births [in the United States] and have a great deal of control, essentially a monopoly, over the maternity care system. Obstetricians are taught to view birth in a medical framework rather than to understand it as a natural process. In a medical model, pregnancy and birth are illnesses that require diagnosis and treatment. It is an obstetrician's job to figure out what's wrong (diagnosis) and do something about it (treatment)—even though, with childbirth, the right thing in most cases is to do nothing. To put it another way, having an obstetrical surgeon manage a normal birth is like having a pediatric surgeon babysit a normal two-year-old. Both will find medical solutions to normal situations—drugs to stimulate normal labor and narcotics for a fussy toddler. It's a paradigm that doesn't work.*

Once the hospital gown is on, the usual next step is to climb into bed. This denies Mother the body's ability to progress through labor in a normal fashion, as it was designed to do utilizing the stimulation of movement and gravity. Food is almost always withheld, except perhaps some ice chips, and needed calories and fluids are replaced with an intravenous drip for hydration. Childbirth Educators describe what is known as the "cascade of interventions" that has now begun. If a mother doesn't start labor when someone on the hospital staff thinks she should or arrives at the hospital in the course of normal labor and does not "progress" well (per hospital protocol expectations), all too often Pitocin (artificial oxytocin) or perhaps worse yet, Cytotec is administered to help increase the strength of contractions and to speed up the labor process. Cytotec has not been approved by either the drug manufacturer or the FDA for that purpose. It is given to "ripen the cervix" and begin the onset of labor. Use of this particular drug increases the risk of uterine rupture, particularly if the woman has had a previous c-section where a weakness to the uterine wall already exists. (Wagner, 2006) When the intensity of the contractions caused by this external force becomes too difficult for the mother to bear, she is asked if she'd like something to help cope with the pain, an epidural (an intravenously administered narcotic cocktail) being one of the most frequent offerings.

After the spinal administration of the epidural, the mother is rarely able to move about. She is confined to bed and generally must remain in the lithotomic position—flat on her back. This position is notorious for putting the mother's body in a situation where the circulation to her lower extremities is compromised and the baby must be pushed "uphill" against gravity. Additionally, having an epidural is linked with a number of potentially dangerous outcomes (see table).

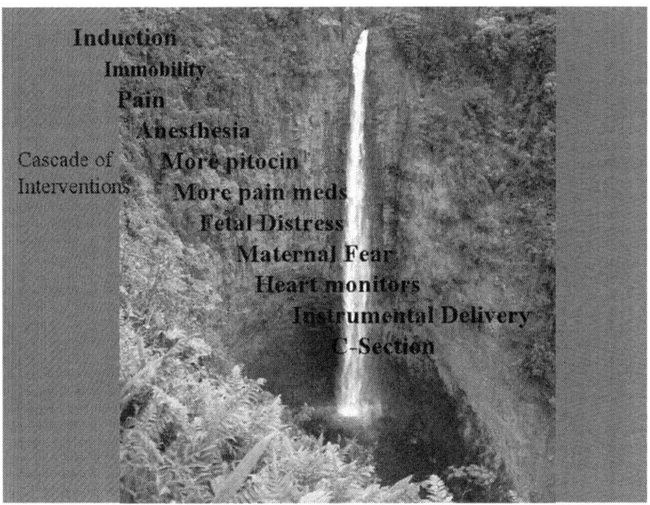

These drugs and poor positioning often lead to problems with the baby's heart rate and/or the slowing of labor. For the baby, the use of narcotics at this stage can have some very far-reaching effects. As the brain takes the narcotic straight to his brain's pleasure center, a ready-made pathway is created for any future drug experimentation. (Karr-Morse and Wiley, 1997) Studies show that the use of typical labor drugs is a possible cause of subtle alterations in the formation of synapses, neurons, and neural transmitters that may be undetectable at birth but surface later as problems with motor development and behavioral issues. (Karr-Morse and Wiley, 1997)

In the course of normal vaginal birth, a baby is gradually compressed by the mother's uterus and pushed down the birth canal and out into the world. As the baby's lungs are compressed, the excess fluids that have built up in his lungs are expelled through his mouth and nose. By contrast, a baby born via Cesarean section without the experience of this compression retains those fluids and is at much higher risk for respiratory issues such as pneumonia shortly after birth. (Wagner, 2006)

As hospital births began replacing home births by the end of the Second World War, women began to relinquish more and more control of their bodies and all that happened to them to hospital-controlled environments. Early hospital births were lonely experiences where women suffered any number of humiliating experiences. Upon admission to the labor ward, women were deprived of their clothes and given a hospital gown, their pubic hair was then shaved, and an enema was administered. Most often a woman would labor in solitary, lying alone in bed, denied food and water.

Without support and companionship, pain would be exacerbated by fear and the woman would feel unable to cope with the labor her body was experiencing. For pain relief a variety of pain medications were available, most commonly meperidine (Demerol) injections or a combination of morphine (a narcotic) plus scopolamine (an amnesiac) which resulted in "twilight sleep." Mothers who were drugged during the pushing phase of birth were unable to participate in delivering their babies, which led to increases in the use of forceps and vacuum extraction on their babies. While the use of these techniques might be necessary to help extract a baby where there are problems in the delivery, they are not without risk to the baby.

More recently, epidurals, (a narcotic cocktail of medications administered through the lumbar vertebrae space in a woman's spine) have become more widely used and are in many cases the expected standard of treatment. The purpose of administering an epidural is to block the pain receptors in the abdominal area so that a woman has no sensation there of pain or anything else during the final stages of labor. An advantage of this method over many of the previously used modern methods is that the mother is able to remain completely conscious during her birth. The downside is that she must now be confined to bed since she may have no sensation from the waist down.

If that is all that occurred, this might not be such a bad thing. However, in addition to not feeling pain sensations, the other communications of the woman's body that help to control the progress of labor via her highly sophisticated endocrine system are disconnected from her birthing experience. Also, the intense physical need to bear down, push and help deliver her baby is impaired if the epidural is still active. Without the feedback sensation from her body, how does a woman know how to work with her own body and baby to know exactly when and how hard to push to help her baby's entry into the world? If she is unable to push appropriately, the care provider may have to make a surgical cut of her vagina (an episiotomy) to enlarge the space, or use forceps or vacuum extraction. Epidural anesthesia is used in up to 90% of some US hospitals. Originally thought to be a very low risk form of pain relief, studies show that it its use is far from harmless.

The use of epidural anesthesia leads to a 15 to 20% increase in maternal fever, which can require medications and invasive treatments. Epidurals do not always work either. Ten percent of epidurals administered provide no pain relief. Sometimes, the numbing does not occur in the expected abdominal region but in the legs; or, only one side of the mother's body is numb while the other side feels each contraction. Back pain after birth is seen in up to one-third of women using epidural anesthesia.

Interventions and Outcomes

When forces outside the mother's body change the normal birth process the baby may have to contend with a uterus that ceases to function properly because the mechanism that guides the rotation of the baby as it descends through the birth canal can be adversely affected by an epidural block. This can lead to baby being forcibly dragged out of his comfortable environment into the world by use of forceps or vacuum extraction. Forceps can cause bruising and damage to the trigeminal nerve in the infant's cranium, which has connections to the palate, tongue, lower jaw, and nose. Vacuum assistance has been reported to nearly always cause a subdermal (under the skin) hematoma, or bruise. Subaponeurotica (a disconnection of the fibrous tissue under the skin of the cranium) or nerve inflammation hematoma happens when veins are damaged and blood accumulates in the space between the nerve and the skull. "Since the subaponeurotic space has no containing membranes or no boundaries, the hematoma may extend from the orbital ridges (above the eyes) to the nape of the neck. This condition is dangerous because of the large potential space for blood accumulation and the possibility of life-threatening hemorrhage." (Kroeger, 2004), In addition to the baby's aching head, the hematoma also substantially raises the baby's risk of fetal distress, postpartum jaundice, and poor neurological function at one month of age.(IBID, 2004)

The nerve damage of vacuum extraction or use of forceps can be either temporary or permanent. It is common to see babies who were products of assisted deliveries that are unable to coordinate their suck, swallow, and breathing functions. This scenario can make successful feedings difficult or impossible. The outcome for babies and their mothers is often premature weaning from the breast.

As if that weren't enough, nearly a quarter of all mothers receiving epidurals have some type of complication, including death. The risk of death during childbirth is tripled for a mother receiving an epidural. (Wagner, 2006) One out of five will be temporarily paralyzed from a few hours up to several days following the administration of epidural anesthesia. One in every 500,000 will experience permanent paralysis. Besides paralysis, 15% to 20% of mothers will develop a fever following an epidural block administration. Both maternal and infant fevers require a "work–up" (per hospital protocols) to rule out an infection. Some of the procedures involved may be quite invasive, including doing a spinal tap on the baby—a painful procedure with its own inherent risks. Mothers are often told to discontinue breastfeeding because of an undiagnosed fever, even though this is contrary to the Academy of Breastfeeding Medicine's protocols (*ABM Clinical Protocol #5: Peripartum Breastfeeding Management for the Healthy Mother and Infant at Term, Revision, June 2008.)*

http://www.bfmed.org/Media/Files/Protocols/Protocol_5.pdf

Another complication suffered by 15 % to 35% of women following epidural anesthesia is urinary retention (the inability to urinate.) If this persists, it can lead to the not-so-pleasant placement of a catheter into the bladder until its function returns. (Wagner, 2006)

One of the possible outcomes of epidural anesthesia is the deceleration of labor and a longer second stage of labor. When an epidural is administered, the likelihood is four times greater that instrumental extraction by forceps or vacuum will be implemented than when no medication is given. The administration of an epidural also doubles the likelihood of cesarean delivery. (Wagner, 2006) Part of the reason for this result is that an epidural blocks the mechanism in mother's body that guides the rotation of the fetus as it descends down the birth canal. Because of this interference in the process, there is a greater chance that the baby will wind up in a position that is more difficult for birth—for example, the posterior position in which the baby is facing the wrong way during his decent. A poor position is apt to be more stressful for the baby and also increases the possibility of more interventions being performed, putting the baby and mother at even greater risk. If the baby can't be delivered vaginally because he hasn't descended properly, then there is a high probability an emergency cesarean section will be performed.

At a recent birth, the mother was reassured that the analgesic (epidural) would not affect her labor. Immediately after its administration her baby's heart rate dropped precipitously, not an uncommon occurrence. (Wagner, 2006) She wasn't able to feel her body's urge to push because she was numb (due to the analgesic), and when the time came to push, she had no sensation to help her participate in getting her baby down the birth canal. This necessitated the use of vacuum extraction because the baby wasn't finished descending all the way, and because the baby's heart rate had dropped time was of the essence.

As a result of some protracted vacuum assistance, even with an episiotomy to enlarge the vaginal opening the baby was born with a huge hematoma. When seen at ten days of age, the poor baby's head was still very tender and she was sporting a raised bruise with a diameter larger than that of a softball. By that point the baby had learned some very poor eating habits and required a fair amount of retraining. The situation didn't resolve completely until the hematoma had abated a week or so later.

We can only imagine how difficult it was for the baby to try to learn all the tasks of a newborn with a major headache complicating the process for days or weeks. The unnecessary pain and suffering of that family, not to mention the expense incurred to try to rectify the problems, was quite avoidable.

The Cesarean rate in the United States now exceeds 30%. Considering that it was under 5% in 1965 and our outcomes have only negligibly improved, this practice warrants a red flag! The World Health Organization (WHO) states that no region in the world is justified in having a cesarean rate greater than 10-15%. Many hospitals in the United States are also reporting upwards of 90% of all mothers receiving epidurals and/or inductions. Surely mothers and babies have not experienced a high enough rate of genetic alteration in just forty years to create a legitimate need for this!

Birth is a life process that—if not interfered with—goes well far more often than not. Indeed, it is wonderful that we have the technical expertise to intervene when necessary. But all too often interventions become iatrogenic (medically induced) causes for poor outcomes, even death.

If epidural anesthesia creates problems for mothers, does it harm babies? One of the reasons that most mothers feel comfortable with using epidural anesthesia is that they believe it to be harmless to their babies. Indeed, that was initially thought at the advent of the use of routine epidurals, and frequently mothers are *still* told the epidurals will not hurt their babies. Care providers frequently do not provide mothers with information on the possible risks of having an epidural. Even though a mother may sign an informed consent form, often she is not in a frame of mind to either read or understand the risks and so no clear information is provided with the time and information to process the ramifications of the procedure. As time goes on and the impact of epidurals is studied, it appears that they are *not* as innocuous as previously thought. A study by Sepkowski et al noted that mothers who received epidurals were found to have labors of longer duration, more oxytocin (Pitocin) augmentation, and more instrumental deliveries–none of which are better circumstances for babies.

In addition, several studies point to the conclusion that labor anesthesia (epidural) "disturbs a natural behavior sequence of newborn breast-seeking behavior, adding to the evidence already discussed" in the works of Rigard, Nissen *et al*, and others. In a 2003 prospective study by Baumgartner *et al*, in two equivalent groups of 115 vaginal delivery groups–one receiving epidural anesthesia and the other no medication during delivery—the results in terms of successful breastfeeding were notable. The group whose mothers had received epidural anesthesia had 69.6% successful breastfeeding behavior compared to 81% of babies whose mothers delivered without epidurals. Additionally, the babies whose mothers had epidurals were more likely to receive a supplementary bottle of formula during their hospital stay. (Kroeger, 2004) Apparently, mothers who trusted their bodies to birth their babies were more likely to trust their bodies to feed their children following birth.

These iatrogenic *(medically caused)* problems resulting from protocols and practices that are not evidence-based create more unnecessary testing, and more risks associated with testing. The more we interfere with the course of a normal birth, the greater the likelihood of adverse side effects. Problems that are caused by medical personnel or procedures are called iatrogenic disorders. Many birth complications are therefore iatrogenic in nature.*(An iatrogenic disorder is a condition that is caused by medical personnel or procedures or that develops through exposure to the environment of a health care facility. Mosby's Medical Dictionary, 8th edition. © 2009, Elsevier.)*

After administration of the epidural, there is frequently a sudden drop in blood flow to the fetus through the placenta. This can result in mild to severe lack of oxygen to the fetus with the potential of brain damage to the baby. This would certainly create a scenario in which the baby would need to be delivered as soon as possible–either by an emergency C-section or, if the baby was sufficiently descended down the birth canal, with an episiotomy and vacuum assist to bring the baby into the world. Neither is generally what mother anticipated the experience would be.

What about the use of the surgical procedure of episiotomy or cutting the vaginal opening during childbirth)? Are there any drawbacks to this very common procedure performed on 70% to 80% of mothers with their first births? (Wagner, 2006) In fact, there are a number of distressing connections to this practice. The premise for performing an episiotomy seems sound-—to prevent excessive 3rd and 4th degree vaginal or even vaginal--rectal lacerations, to prevent long-term damage to the woman's pelvic floor, and to protect the baby from an extended labor. The problem is that none of these is supported by evidence. Experts in the field feel that an episiotomy rate of 5-10 % is more appropriate than the routine performance so often seen.

It was originally thought that an incision would heal easier than a tear of the skin. However, when a tear occurs, the skin separates unevenly, sort of like fingers that can be put back in place similar to puzzle pieces, and it can heal much faster and with a significant reduction in pain. A running stitch used to just hold the sides of the tear together reconnects easily and heals rapidly. By contrast, the tight stitches that are frequently used to sew up an episiotomy can be very painful since they are all that hold the wound together. Many mothers have reported feeling intense pain in the perineal area following an episotomy that can last up to a year or more after birth. Episiotomy is also responsible for a 53% increase in painful sexual intercourse, as well as doubling the woman's risk of fecal incontinence.

Women's expectation that they will labor and deliver in the lithotomy position with the mother lying on her back with her legs spread and elevated is notorious for compromising the circulation to her lower extremities. Bodies work best for giving birth when they are able to use the natural forces of gravity by being vertical—standing, sitting or squatting. The pelvic floor is able to open most fully when the mother is squatting. A wider opening would reduce the necessity for a surgical procedure like an episiotomy.

A study done in 1979 by Dr. Caldeyro-Barcia of Uruguay found that the duration of first stage labor for vertical mothers was 36% shorter than that of mothers in horizontal positions. In addition, mothers giving birth in vertical positions reported less pain, less fetal hypoxia (deficiency of oxygen), less acidosis (fetal distress), and the incidence of infant head molding was reduced. (Kroger, 2004)

There have been any number of high-tech adjustable birthing beds and chairs, but none have been as malleable as a simple bean bag chair which the mother can mold to support herself in the ways that feel right to her with a minimum of effort on her part. So why isn't something like this utilized? One significant reason is that it would put the attending care provider physically lower than the mother down on the floor. That's just not going to happen. (Wagner, 2006)

Following the Birth—What happens to the Baby?

We often hear a mother tell us, "Thank heaven I was in a hospital. They saved my baby's life when his heart rate decelerated." It seldom dawns on her at that time that the baby's heart would have been just fine had it not been for the interventions initiated by the hospital policies or medical orders.

To add insult to injury, infants are frequently systematically removed from their mothers moments after birth as a second cascade of interventions is initiated. Mother, the only constant in the baby's life, goes missing at this most critical time. There is no rationale for this separation. Mothers are told that the infant needs to be weighed and measured, then "checked" by the attending nurse to be sure everything is satisfactory. Why can't this inspection happen while baby is on mother's body? Why can't he be weighed and checked along with the requisite prophylactic eye treatment and Vitamin K injection after he is in his recovery sleep a scant hour or two following birth?

Research has shown that delaying these "eyes and thighs" procedures by a few hours has no negative impact on the baby. With just this slight change in the protocols and procedures, a newborn would be able to see and experience life outside of the womb in his first hour with his parents without getting poked and prodded as he's trying figure out this whole new environment. Ironically, we wouldn't dream of taking the puppies or kittens of our pets away from their mothers right after birth. Why don't we think our babies deserve at least the same consideration given our pets?

At birth the baby is has a biological expectation to get acquainted with his parents, especially Mom. All at once, with a clip of his umbilical cord his continuous feeding system has been removed. The constant temperature control of the womb is gone and suddenly he feels chilly—where is mother to fix it all? Then there are those new lungs to be inflated; he's now responsible to get his own oxygen. With the severing of the umbilical cord comes the requisite learning of how to adapt to an entirely different set of circumstances to survive this new world. Now the newborn must find his own food while learning how to coordinate the processes of sucking, swallowing, and breathing. When a baby is removed from his expected "habitat," his mother, panic ensues. For him, separation is akin to death. "Where is my mother?" he shrieks as the staff speaks reassuringly to her about what great lungs he has. It's been said that crying is good for the lungs, but it would be more appropriate to equating it to bleeding being good for the veins.

Supplementation of the Breastfed Baby

"Just One Bottle Won't Hurt"---or Will It?

Marsha Walker, RN, IBCLC

Background

- The gastrointestinal (GI) tract of a normal fetus is sterile
- the type of delivery has an effect on the development of the intestinal microbiota

  - vaginally born infants are colonized with their mother's bacteria
  - cesarean born infants' initial exposure is more likely to environmental microbes from the air, other infants, and the nursing staff which serves as vectors for transfer
  - the primary gut flora in infants born by cesarean delivery may be disturbed for up to 6 months after birth (Gronlund et al, 1999)
- babies at highest risk of colonization by undesirable microbes or when transfer from maternal sources cannot occur are cesarean-delivered babies, preterm infants, full term infants requiring intensive care, or infants separated from their mother
  - infants requiring intensive care acquire intestinal organisms slowly and the establishment of bifidobacterial flora is retarded
  - a delayed bacterial colonization of the gut with a limited number of bacterial species tends to be virulent
  - control and manipulation of the neonatal gut with human milk can be used as a strategy to prevent and treat intestinal diseases (Dai & Walker, 1999)
- major ecological disturbances are observed in newborn infants treated with antimicrobial agents
  - one way of minimizing ecological disturbances in the NICU is to provide these babies with fresh breast milk (Zetterstrom et al, 1994)
- breastfed and formula-fed infants have different gut flora
  - breastfed babies have a lower gut pH (acidic environment) of approximately 5.1-5.4 throughout the first six weeks that is dominated by bifidobacteria with reduced pathogenic (disease-causing) microbes such as *E coli, bacteroides, clostridia, and streptococci*
  - flora with a diet-dependent pattern is present from the 4th day of life with breast milk-fed guts showing a 47% bifidobacterium and formula-fed guts showing 15%. Enterococci prevail in formula-fed infants (Rubaltelli et al, 1998)

   - babies fed formula have a high gut pH of approximately 5.9-7.3 with a variety of putrefactive bacterial species
   - in infants fed breast milk and formula supplements the mean pH is approximately 5.7-6.0 during the first four weeks, falling to 5.45 by the sixth week
   - when formula supplements are given to breastfed babies during the first seven days of life, the production of a strongly acidic environment is delayed and its full potential may never be reached
   - breastfed infants who receive supplements develop gut flora and behavior like formula-fed infants
- The neonatal GI tract undergoes rapid growth and maturational change following birth
   - Infants have a functionally immature and immunonaive gut at birth
   - Tight junctions of the GI mucosa take many weeks to mature and close the gut to whole proteins and pathogens
   - Intestinal permeability decreases faster in breastfed babies than in formula-fed infants (Catassi, et al, 1995)
   - Open junctions and immaturity play a role in the acquisition of NEC, diarrheal disease, and allergy
   - sIgA from colostrum and breast milk coats the gut, passively providing immunity during the time of reduced neonatal gut immune function
   - mothers' sIgA is antigen specific. The antibodies are targeted against pathogens in the baby's immediate surroundings
   - the mother synthesizes antibodies when she ingests, inhales, or otherwise comes in contact with a disease-causing microbe
   - these antibodies ignore useful bacteria normally found in the gut and ward off disease without causing inflammation
- infant formula should not be given to a breastfed baby before gut closure occurs

- o once dietary supplementation begins, the bacterial profile of breastfed infants resembles that of formula-fed infants in which bifidobacteria are no longer dominant and the development of obligate anaerobic bacterial populations occurs (Mackie, Sghir, Gaskins, 1999)
- o relatively small amounts of formula supplementation of breastfed infants (one supplement per 24 hours) will result in shifts from a breastfed to a formula-fed gut flora pattern (Bullen, Tearle, Stewart, 1977)
- o the introduction of solid food to the breastfed infant causes a major perturbation in the gut ecosystem, with a rapid rise in the number of enterobacteria and enterococci, followed by a progressive colonization by bacteroides, clostridia, and anaerobic streptococci (Stark & Lee, 1982)
- o with the introduction of supplementary formula, the gut flora in a breastfed baby becomes almost indistinguishable from normal adult flora within 24 hours (Gerstley, Howell, Nagel, 1932)
- o if breast milk were again given exclusively, it would take 2-4 weeks for the intestinal environment to return again to a state favoring the gram-positive flora (Brown & Bosworth, 1922; Gerstley, Howell, Nagel, 1932)

- in susceptible families, breastfed babies can be sensitized to cow's milk protein by the giving of just one bottle, (inadvertent supplementation, unnecessary supplementation, or planned supplements), in the newborn nursery during the first three days of life (Host, Husby, Osterballe, 1988; Host, 1991). Small doses of allergens in the newborn nursery should be avoided to prevent allergic manifestations when subsequently challenged with cow's milk (Cantani & Micera, 2005)
    - o infants at high risk of developing atopic disease has been calculated at 37% if one parent has atopic disease, 62-85% if both parents are affected and dependant on whether the parents have similar or dissimilar clinical disease, and those infants showing elevated levels of IgE in cord blood irrespective of family history (Chandra, 2000)

- o cross reactivity exists between cow's milk protein and human milk protein (Bernard et al, 2000). Only 1 nanogram of bovine b-lactoalbumin is required to sensitize a susceptible infant (Businco et al, 1999)
- o in breastfed infants at risk, hypoallergenic formulas can be used to supplement breastfeeding; solid foods should not be introduced until 6 months of age, dairy products delayed until 1 year of age, and the mother should consider eliminating peanuts, tree nuts, cow's milk, eggs, and fish from her diet (Zieger, 1999; AAP, 2000)
- o stored frozen breast milk is the optimal choice for supplementing a breastfed baby, especially in the presence of high atopic risk; in the absence of stored breast milk, an extensively (not partially) protein hydrolyzed formula is recommended (Zeiger, 2003)
- o study results on asthma and atopy can be confounded by the early introduction of infant formula, as small amounts of early formula may be damaging to the development of an infant's immune system; this should be considered in research analysis, even if a mother goes on to predominantly breastfeed (Oddy et al, 2003)

- in susceptible families, early exposure to cow's milk proteins can increase the risk of the infant or child developing insulin dependent diabetes mellitus (IDDM) (Mayer et al, 1988; Karjalainen, et al, 1992)
  - o human insulin content in breast milk is significantly higher than bovine insulin in cow's milk; insulin content in infant formulas is extremely low to absent; insulin supports gut maturation
  - o in animal models oral administration of human insulin stimulates the intestinal immune system generating active cellular mechanisms that suppress the development of autoimmune diabetes
  - o the lack of human insulin in infant formulas may break the tolerance to insulin and lead to the development of type 1 diabetes (Vaarala et al, 1998)

- o the avoidance of cow's milk protein for the first several months of life may reduce the later development of IDDM or delay its onset in susceptible individuals (AAP, 1994)
- o infants who are exclusively breastfed for at least 4 months have a lower risk of seroconversion leading to beta-cell autoimmunity
    - short-term breastfeeding and the early introduction of cow's milk based infant formula predispose young children who are genetically susceptible to Type 1 diabetes to progressive signs of beta-cell autoimmunity (Kimpimaki et al, 2001)
- o sensitization and development of immune memory to cow's milk protein is the initial step in the etiology of IDDM (Kostraba, et al, 1993)
    - sensitization can occur with very early exposure to cow's milk before gut cellular tight junction closure
    - sensitization can occur with exposure to cow's milk during an infection-caused gastrointestinal alteration when the mucosal barrier is compromised allowing antigens to cross and initiate immune reactions
    - sensitization can occur if the presence of cow's milk protein in the gut damages the mucosal barrier, inflames the gut, destroys binding components of cellular junctions, or other early insult with cow's milk protein leads to sensitization (Savilahti, et al, 1993)
- o beta cell autoimmunity is increased in children who are not breastfed or breastfed for a short time. Early introduction of cow's milk based formula increases the risk for developing type 1 diabetes up to 5 years of age in the general population (Holmberg et al, 2007)

The Nutritional Committees from the American Academy of Pediatrics and jointly the European Society for Pediatric Allergology and Clinical Immunology and the European Society for Pediatric Gastroenterology, Hepatology, and Nutrition recommend exclusive breastfeeding as the hallmark for food allergy prevention (Zeiger, 2003; Muraro, et al, 2004))

References

American Academy of Pediatrics, Work Group on Cow's Milk Protein and Diabetes Mellitus. Infant feeding practices and their possible relationship to the etiology of diabetes mellitus. Pediatrics 1994; 94:752-754

American Academy of Pediatrics, Committee on Nutrition. Hypoallergenic infant formulas. Pediatrics 2000; 106:346-349

Bernard H et al. Molecular basis of IgE cross-reactivity between human beta-casein and bovine beta-casein, a major allergy in milk. Mol Immunol 2000; 37:161-167

Brown EW, Bosworth AW. Studies of infant feeding VI. A bacteriological study of the feces and the food of normal babies receiving breast milk. Am J Dis Child 1922; 23:243

Bullen CL, Tearle PV, Stewart MG. The effect of humanized milks and supplemented breast feeding on the faecal flora of infants. J Med Microbiol 1977; 10:403-413

Businco L, Bruno G, Giampietro PG. Prevention and management of food allergy. Acta Paediatr Suppl (430) 1999; 88:104-109

Cantani A, Micera M. Neonatal cow milk sensitization in 143 case-reports: role of early exposure to cow's milk formula. European Rev Medical Pharnacological Sciences 2005; 9:227-230

Catassi C, et al. Intestinal permeability changes during the first month: effect of natural versus artificial feeding. J Pediatr Gastroenterol Nutr 1995; 21:383-386

Chandra RK. Food allergy and nutrition in early life: implications for later health. Proc Nutr Soc 2000; 59:273-277

Dai D, Walker WA. Protective nutrients and bacterial colonization in the immature human gut. Adv Pediatr 1999; 46:353-382

Gerstley JR, Howell KM, Nagel BR. Some factors influencing the fecal flora of infants. Am J Dis Child 1932; 43:555

Gronlund MM, et al. Fecal microflora in healthy infants born by different methods of delivery: permanent changes in intestinal flora after cesarean delivery. J Pediatr Gastroenterol Nutr 1999; 28:19-25

Holmberg H, Wahlberg J, Vaarala O, et al. Short duration of breastfeeding as a risk factor for B-cell autoantibodies in 5 year old children from the general population. Br J Nutr 2007; 97:111-116

Host A, Husby S, Osterballe O. A prospective study of cow's milk allergy in exclusively breastfed infants. Acta Paediatr Scand 1988; 77:663-670

Host A. Importance of the first meal on the development of cow's milk allergy and intolerance. Allergy Proc 1991; 10:227-232

Karjalainen J, Martin JM, Knip M, et al. A bovine albumin peptide as a possible trigger of insulin-dependent diabetes mellitus. N Engl J Med 1992; 327:302-307

Kimpimaki T, et al. Short-term exclusive breastfeeding predisposes young children with increased genetic risk of Type 1 diabetes to progressive beta-cell autoimmunity. Diabetologia 2001; 44:63-69

Kostraba JN, Cruickshanks KJ, Lawler-Heavner J, et al. Early exposure to cow's milk and solid foods in infancy, genetic predisposition, and risk of IDDM. Diabetes 1993; 42:288-295

Mackie RI, Sghir A, Gaskins HR. Developmental microbial ecology of the neonatal gastrointestinal tract. Am J Clin Nutr 1999; 69(Suppl):1035S-1045S

Mayer EJ, Hamman RF, Gay EC, et al. Reduced risk of IDDM among breastfed children. The Colorado IDDM Registry. Diabetes 1988; 37:1625-1632

Muraro A, Dreborg S, Halken S, et al. Dietary prevention of allergic diseases in infants and small children. Part III: Critical review of published peer-reviewed observational and interventional studies and final recommendations. Pediatr Allergy Immunol 2004; 15:291-307

Oddy WH, Peat JK. Breastfeeding, asthma, and atopic disease: an epidemiological review of the literature. J Hum Lact 2003; 19:250-261

Rubaltelli FF, et al. Intestinal flora in breast and bottle-fed infants. J Perinat Med 1998; 26:186-191

Savilahti E, Tuomilehto J, Saukkonen TT, et al. Increased levels of cow's milk and b-lactoglobulin antibodies in young children with newly diagnosed IDDM. Diabetes Care 1993; 16:984-989

Stark PL, Lee A. The microbial ecology of the large bowel of breastfed and formula-fed infants during the first year of life. J Med Microbiol 1982; 15:189-203

Vaarala O, et al. Cow milk feeding induces antibodies to insulin in children – a link between cow milk and insulin-dependent mellitus? Scand J Immunol 1998; 47:131-135

Zetterstrom R, et al. Early infant feeding and micro-ecology of the gut. Acta Paediatr Jpn 1994; 36:562-571

Zieger R. Prevention of food allergy in infants and children. Immunology & Allergy Clinics of North America 1999; 19(3)

Zeiger RS. Food allergen avoidance in the prevention of food allergy in infants and children. Pediatrics 2003; 111:1662-1671 (Suppl)

Used with permission, Marsha Walker, RN, IBCLC.

This is a very common scenario played out in countless U.S. hospitals every day. The world our little Stone Age baby arrives in is not the world he is biologically programmed to expect and in which he can survive and thrive.

For eons, in all parts of the world women gave birth without the routine use of anesthesia. In maternity hospitals in underdeveloped countries with limited resources, as well as in home birth and birth center facilities, there are other means of helping mothers cope with the pain resulting from the work of giving birth. Rather than attempting to mask or obliterate the sensations caused by labor, women are showed how to work with the contractions and to open up their bodies in preparation for their child's birth. Comfort measures such as controlled breathing, massage, positioning, movement, hydrotherapy, prayers, and chanting are used to move through the progression of labor to the delivery of the baby.

When our first ancestors gave birth in millennia past, the event would take place in a small space with few attendants, low light levels, and privacy. If one has ever witnessed a domesticated mammal giving birth, such as a dog or cat, they have seen the mother prepare her birth area. She makes a safe nest/space where she can feel free to bring her offspring into the world. When the "nest" is complete she generally will go into labor, culminating with the birth of her litter. Her work is often more silent than loud when she can respond to the rhythms of her own body and move in ways that facilitate the babies' journey down the birth canal. After birth, the babies move to find the teats and their mother's milk. Baby mammals know how to find their food. Human newborns are just as capable of crawling to their mother's breast with a reflex known as stepping motions, which has been well documented.(Righard, 1990) When a healthy, full-term human baby reaches the breast, the instinctive behavior to open wide and latch on to mother's breast is quite fully intact. (Smillie, 2010)

In nonhospital settings as labor became more intense and led to birth, the mother would squat on her own or with assistance from a helper in order to maximize the pelvic floor opening and facilitate as easy a birth as possible. As the baby's head begins to emerge (crown) through the opening of the birth canal, the mother or attendant would reach down to support the baby as he completed his journey into the world. After entering into the extrauterine world, the new infant would be brought into his mother's arms and onto her chest to rest, recover, and begin his adventure outside of the womb. At his mother's breast, he found all he needed—warmth, the sounds of the familiar rhythms of her body, her love, and her milk. Being skin to skin made everything right in his new little world outside the womb.

Why Is Skin-to-Skin So Important?

Being continuously close to his mother's body in skin-to skin contact immediately after birth is the expectation of a human infant. It is the same for any primate. Although many hospitals are now encouraging mothers to have a "Golden Hour" following birth to hold their baby "skin to skin," this is a *process*, not a single event. Even though the nurse may be able to check off the box that "skin-to-skin" has been completed, this is just the beginning as far as the baby is concerned.

Skin-to-skin contact immediately after birth is important for colonizing the baby with his mother's bacteria. Along with breastfeeding, this can be helpful in the prevention of allergic diseases. When babies are placed into incubators they are colonized by bacteria different from the mothers'. In addition, skin-to-skin contact helps with thermoregulation (keeping the body temperature within an appropriate range). If Baby's temperature drops, Mother's temperature can respond by increasing a full 2 degrees centigrade if necessary to provide sufficient warmth to her child. Additionally, if her baby gets too warm, she can reduce her own body temperature by a full degree in response to her baby's needs. This maintains efficient respiratory patterns and oxygen saturation and reduces apnea (temporary cessation of breathing) and bradycardia (a slow heartbeat—pulse rate under sixty beats per minute). SSC helps increase infant weight gain and maternal milk production. It also can serve as an analgesic during painful medical procedures. Mothers who nurse their babies during routine vaccination administration report that the babies barely notice. This is true even during a spinal tap, very painful procedure generally done without any analgesia.

Keeping baby skin to skin helps him maintain his heart rate and blood pressure. His blood sugar levels are higher, and he is less likely to cry. SSC has found to be associated with greater likelihood of exclusive breastfeeding and extensive breastfeeding. Healthy People 2010 set the goals for breastfeeding in the U.S. to 80% of all babies born breastfeeding initially, 50% still to be breastfeeding at six months, and 25% still breastfeeding by their first birthday. These recommendations are consistent with those of the American Academy of Pediatrics (AAP) and World Health Organization (WHO).

The new Healthy People 2020: Breastfeeding Objectives are for 81.9% of all infants to be breastfed initially, 60.6% still to be breastfeeding at six months, and 34.1% at one year of age. (*U.S. Department of Health and Human Services, 2011)*

Perhaps one of the best outcomes of SSC is its positive impact on the mother's sense of competence and its enhancement of the mother-baby attachment/bonding process. When mothers begin their maternal journey empowered, they are able to cope with the trials and tribulations of raising children much more confidently than if they are unsure about what they are doing.

Babies held close to their mothers have access to their warm, nourishing milk and protection from the outside world. Babies are close enough to eat when hungry and seldom need to cry to communicate their needs. They ought to be considered extensions of their mothers for much of the first extrauterine year, until they can get about on their own.

Our modern baby is instead in a nursery "exercising his lungs," calling for a mother who is unable to hear him as she lies in her room down the hall. Though her body would stabilize both his heart and breathing rates, as well as providing all the necessary hydration, nutrients, immunities, and comfort he needs, he is instead being poked, prodded, and ignored. He is often filled with "food" (formula) that is frequently given in quantities larger than his stomach capacity (about 5 -7 ml – the size of a marble - on the first day of life.) This "food" disrupts his ability to fight infection and may trigger lifelong allergies, as well as interfering with him learning how to access the breast for the nutrition that he needs. (*Walker, 2007*)

When reunited with Mother, sometimes Baby doesn't take to the breast. If his first meal was artificial infant milk (formula) from a bottle, the quantity of liquid and the manner of sucking required with a bottle may now make it difficult to do what he likely would have done well without any interference. "Sucking" from a bottle and "suckling" a breast require very different skills. Sucking is the use of negative pressure such as one might use to draw liquid through a straw into one's mouth. It is the mechanism that babies use when transferring liquid from a bottle. Infant suckling is a much more complex process that involves using the jaw to compress the breast and using the tongue in a peristaltic wave-like motion to transfer milk from the breast. The processes are similar, but not interchangeable. Trying to teach a baby how to suckle a breast and suck on a bottle is like trying to teach them how to play American football and soccer on the same day—the result is often a great deal of confusion or inability to do either skill well.

Add to this a little person who has been affected by the drugs from labor, and the stage is set for problems. The baby's urge to seek out the breast may be overwhelmed by sensations of sleepiness. The early bottle may be confusing his instinctive ability to latch on to his mother's breast. If he was also bathed immediately after his birth, the amniotic fluid that was on his hands would be washed off. The scent of the amniotic fluid is very similar to the secretions of the mother's Montgomery glands on her areola surrounding the nipple. Under normal circumstances, baby would suck on his hands and seek out the familiar scent at mother's breast. Righard and Adele's study found that:

> *Every newborn, when placed on her mother's abdomen, soon after birth, has the ability to find her mother's breast all on her own and to decide when to take the first breastfeed. This is called the 'Breast Crawl'. It was first described in 1987 at the Karolinska Institute in Sweden (Widström et al, 1987). The description of the Breast Crawl, compiled from the article, is as follows: Immediately after birth the child was dried and laid on the mother's chest. In the control group a regular behavioural sequence, previously not described in the literature, was observed. After 15 minutes of comparative inactivity, spontaneous sucking and rooting movements occurred, reaching maximal intensity at 45 minutes. The first hand-to-mouth movement was observed at a mean of 34± 2 minutes after birth and at 55+ minutes the infant spontaneously found the nipple and started to suckle. These findings suggest that an organized feeding behavior develops in a predictable way during the first hours of life, initially expressed only as spontaneous sucking and rooting movements, soon followed by hand-to-mouth activity together with more intense sucking and rooting activity, and culminating in sucking of the breast.*
>
> http://breastcrawl.org/science.shtml.

Righard and Alade concluded that brief separation of the infant from the mother during the first hour after birth had a strong effect on the success of the first breastfeed, as did medications given during labor (Righard L, Alade MO., 1990). Infants who were both separated and exposed to pethidine/meperidine (Demerol) through their mothers did not breastfed successfully, while almost all those who were neither separated nor exposed to pethidine were successful latching on correctly to their mother's breast. So, the two crucial determinants for a successful start to breastfeeding seem to be uninterrupted contact with the mother until after the first breastfeed and no sedation of the infant by analgesics given to the mother during labor.

Another side effect of such narcotic analgesics as pethidine or butorphanol (Stadol) is central nervous system depression, in both the mother and the infant. The effects of pethidine persist for about 3.0-4.5 hours in the mother, but as long as 13-23 hours in the infant. Reports of respiratory distress or apnea have been reported when butorphanol was administered within two hours of delivery. (Smith, 2010; Wagner, 2006)

Consequently, the infant is depressed for a much longer time than the mother. The plasma concentration of pethidine in the infant is almost as high as that in the mother, reaching a maximum after two to three hours, after which the level falls slowly. In this study, more infants were alert, ready to suckle, and suckled correctly when the time between analgesia and the delivery room was less than two hours than when it was longer.

Separation from the mother to measure and wrap the baby after fifteen to twenty minutes of skin- to-skin contact seriously disturbed the first breastfeeding. That timing seems to be at a very critical stage for separation; just as the infant was about to begin crawling movements, he was removed. The infants generally protested loudly. There is no justifiable reason for routine separation. Measuring and weighing procedures can simply be put off for one to two hours. There is no research to support current customary practices of administration of Vitamin K and eye ointment within the first hour of life. It seems rude that just as the baby is first experiencing a world of vision, limited though it might be, that he should receive an ointment that might sting and will most certainly blur his newfound sense of vision. Although administration of both the eye ointment and the Vitamin K has a scientific basis, the timing does not. Waiting until baby is in his recovery sleep a couple of hours following birth is much less intrusive and yet allows the necessary precautions to be completed by the nursing staff..

Righard and Alade, whose breast crawl video changed perceptions of what babies were capable of recommend:

- The naked infant should be left undisturbed on the mother's abdomen until the first breastfeeding is accomplished, and the infant's efforts to take the breast actively should be encouraged.
- The use of drugs given to the mother during labor should be restricted. (Righard L, Alade MO., 1990)

To allow the Breast Crawl to be successful, (Klaus and Kennel, 2001) strongly urge that the injection of vitamin K, application of eye ointment, washing, and any measuring of infant's height, weight, and head circumference be delayed for at least one hour. In order not to remove the taste and smell of the mother's amniotic fluid, it is necessary to delay washing the baby's hands. The early hand-sucking behavior is markedly reduced when infant is bathed before the crawl.

If mother and baby are separated, if he doesn't breastfeed fairly easily and quickly when the dyad is reunited, his mother may experience this as personal rejection. Or she may be exhausted or traumatized from an overly managed labor and birth. If she has experienced a difficult birth and has been on the receiving end of any of the variety of interventions available, she may have an even greater lack of confidence in the innate abilities of her own body. Often she is simply unaware of the dangers of bottle-feeding artificial milk. So she gives up.

Not only does the baby then miss out on his mother's milk, but he is now being fed a substitute which medical research has proven can lead to many potential problems, including obesity, diabetes and hypertension. He is also being set up for all manner of diseases in both infancy and throughout his lifespan. He will not have the optimal environment to build a healthy attachment to his mother. The biological model requires the context for these things to be breastmilk "direct from the tap," augmented by hours and hours of in-arms relationship with Mother.

Inconsistency of Information

Some mothers, of course, are fiercely determined not to let anything deter their intentions to breastfeed. A mother like this may turn to the doctors and nurses for assistance, sometimes erroneously assuming that they possess expertise in helping her. Some do. Many do not. Often their approach to "helping" is negatively viewed through the lens of their own failed experience or, even more fundamentally, their failure to be current with available research. The nursery nurse especially may think she "owns" the baby during the hospital stay. Some nurses may think either that breastfeeding "management" is their domain as well or perceive it as a challenge to their routine or procedures. Some nurses have limited information about breastfeeding. Some may have personal knowledge because of nursing their own child(ren.) But many nurses—particularly new grads—have limited experience and generally very little education about helping mothers to breastfeed as part of their training. Often hospital policies are outdated and far from evidence based. One of the challenges to hospitals is to update policies and procedures to reflect new evidence-based information. Far too often the existing protocols are based on "the way we've always done it."

The geographical separation of newborn nursery versus postpartum rooms plus the endless parade of visitors may seal the deal on ending breastfeeding. Between widely varied views and lactation helpers (who may or may not be trained and certified—see inset), plus mothers and mothers-in-law with varying degrees of breastfeeding success themselves, the poor new parents are often beset and besieged with a hodgepodge of conflicting, confusing, intimidating advice and information. Add to that the plethora of books and magazine articles based on opinion or misconception, and we should not wonder that parents get a bit lost in the puzzle of feeding their baby.

What is an IBCLC?

The International Board Certified Lactation Consultant (IBCLC) credential identifies a knowledgeable and experienced member of the maternal-child health team who has specialized skills in breastfeeding management and care. The IBLCE certification program offers the only credential in lactation consulting and is available globally.

IBCLCs have passed a rigorous examination that demonstrates the ability to provide competent, comprehensive lactation and breastfeeding care. Attainment of the IBCLC credential signifies that the practitioner has demonstrated competence to:

- work together with mothers to prevent and solve breastfeeding problems
- collaborate with other members of the health care team to provide comprehensive care that supports, protects and promotes breastfeeding
- encourage a social environment that supports breastfeeding families
- educate families, health professionals and policy makers about the far-reaching and long-lasting value of breastfeeding as a global public health imperative.

There are other types of breastfeeding helpers as well. A Lactation Educator, Counselor or Specialist is someone who has completed a 16 hour course and can give basic education about the benefits of breastfeeding but generally lacks the clinical training to help with more challenging issues. There is no formal certification for any level of training other than IBCLC.

Among those who become IBCLCs are nurses, midwives, dietitians, physicians and experienced breastfeeding support counselors. IBCLCs work in a variety of settings including hospitals, clinics, physicians' offices, neonatal intensive care units, human milk banks and private practice.

With a focus on preventive health care, IBCLCs encourage self-care, empowering parents to make their own decisions. IBCLCs use a problem solving approach to provide evidence based information to pregnant and breastfeeding women and make ap-

> propriate referrals to other members of the health care team. The IBLCE has established Professional Standards for IBCLCs and IBCLCs must renew their certification every five years, either through continuing education or by re-examination.

Even if rooming in, few hospitals allow co-sleeping, (having baby sleep with his mother) thereby relegating the baby to the "womb with a view" plastic box, so quaintly named "isolette." And isolation is what babies experience when separated from their mothers. In addition, the possible ongoing effects of labor drugs for both mother and baby make learning even more challenging. Babies are often in some degree of a foggy state for the first three days of life after exposure to labor medications. If mothers are contending with the pain of either a surgical delivery or an episiotomy, the conditions are not exactly fertile for the new mother-baby relationship to grow and thrive.

What hospital teaching is given is often abbreviated, delivered moments before discharge in a didactic manner that the mother's brain, investing all its energies to the very instinctive challenge of mothering, is not able to fully comprehend. (Smillie, 2010) Written instructions might be found days or weeks later. Learning is negligible by that point as experience has colored any general information she may have been given. The baby has changed greatly since leaving the hospital of his birth, and some of the information given at the time of their discharge may not be pertinent to his current state by then.

One of the biggest complaints mothers verbalize is the inconsistency of information they are given about breastfeeding. In hospitals where one nurse is responsible for the baby and another responsible for the mother, there can be four differing opinions if the nurses are working twelve-hour shifts, six if they are working eight-hour shifts.) Needless to say, a fair bit of confusion can occur with so many opinions. While many nurses are quite savvy about breastfeeding and able to offer excellent advice, there are still many who have outdated information or merely their own experience to draw on for their helping skills. This is not exactly the evidence-based information that is expected to be provided to mothers. In no other field of medicine would opinion be passed off as education, but somehow because breastfeeding is considered to be "natural" there is no outrage about the perpetuation of incorrect information.

In most schools of nursing in the United States today, there is little to no formal instruction given to nurses about how to actually help mothers with breastfeeding. It is generally taught that breastfeeding is the recommended method of infant feeding, but the necessary skills to help new mothers are rarely part of the curriculum. Instead, there is plenty of instruction on formula feeding. Most nursing students either have observed or participated in bottle feeding with infant formula since it is still the cultural norm in the USA. So when a mother asks for help in the hospital with breastfeeding, even though the nurse knows that formula feeding is inferior to breastfeeding, s/he feels more confident in the ability to show the mother how to feed her baby formula. It certainly is easier to twist off the cap of the ready-to-feed formula stocked all over the nursery than to try to help teach the mother with skills the nurse was never given. It becomes easier each time to rationalize about how formula is a pretty good substitute and soon it just fits better in the hospital maternal/child ward culture. Mothers often are not aware of the downside of not breastfeeding and just go along with the "professional's" suggestion. Some mothers who have done their research continue to try to figure out how to nurse their baby with or without help and support from the hospital staff.

Another possible problem may be that the staff lactation consultants (or educators) may have differing approaches than the nurses to breastfeeding issues that may arise. Many hospitals have clear policies and protocols with respect to interventions that might be used with a breastfeeding dyad (mother/baby). For example, some hospitals have conflicting information about what to do in case of low blood sugar or may even lack a clear definition of what a low blood sugar might be. Even though the Academy of Breastfeeding information and the Section on Breastfeeding of the American Academy of Pediatrics have clear policies and protocols about various breastfeeding issues/problems and clear treatment plans, they are often underutilized with staff doing "what we've always done" instead of using practices which are evidence based.

http://www.bfmed.org/Resources/Protocols.aspx

The sleepiness of a baby who has received medications during labor and delivery can be problematic since it is expected that they will be eating frequently, at least eight times in a 24-hour period. He may be content to snooze through feedings. This can be complicated by the interruptions from both visitors and hospital staff, making it a somewhat less than ideal situation for mother and baby to learn to breastfeed together. If the hospital still has babies being returned to the nursery, another wedge is placed between mother and baby and learning how to effectively communicate. It is very difficult for Mom to learn baby's signs, signals and cries that communicate his needs if he is down the hall and around the corner from his mother.

Besides mothers trying to separate the chaff from the wheat in the professional information given to them by the hospital staff, new mothers are also often the recipients of the collective wisdom of family and friends. Some of it may be wonderful and full of practical solutions. Far too often the info is fraught with old wives' tales and misinformation. Much of it is fairly harmless, but some is inconsistent with good feeding practices, and some of this so-called advice is quite possibly hazardous to either the baby or mother or both.

On the fairly harmless end of the spectrum is the info about what foods mother should avoid. This is generally comprised of suggestions to avoid spicy or gas-producing foods. Many of these suggestions are without merit. Throughout the course of human history, women have eaten whatever was available in season or whatever foods that could be preserved. Around the equatorial regions, because there was no refrigeration spicy foods helped preserve and keep meats from spoiling. So around the world in those regions, spicy foods are the norm, and mothers in these regions eat the foods of their culture. The babies of those mothers are introduced to the foods of their culture when they're exposed to them first during pregnancy, then via their mothers' milk. Since spicy food is the norm in many cultures and babies do just fine ingesting the foods of their culture, why would spicy foods be considered things mothers should avoid? The reality is that babies rarely care what their mothers eat. The only foods a mother needs to be routinely careful about are known family allergens or food sensitivities on either the maternal or paternal sides, or any food that the baby seems to have an adverse reaction to.

More harmful suggestions might be to give teas and herbs to the newborn baby or to limit the frequency or duration of feedings. Sometimes certain foods are given to the new mother to help bring in a plentiful milk supply. Notions of giving foods other than human milk to babies are fraught with problems, as explained in (Walker, 2007).

Most often the foods offered to new mothers are helpful or neutral with respect to the baby and milk supply. Sometimes soups are made for the new mother but there can be risks of milk suppression with the use of certain cooking herbs such as sage. Another possible harmful contribution is the consumption of large quantities of mint. Both of these herbs have been known to decrease milk supply. (Weed, 1986)

As if conflicting information wasn't enough to confuse the new mother-baby dyad, a new mother is likely to experience somewhere in the neighborhood of 54 interruptions in her 24-hour day at the hospital. A study in the *Journal of Obstetric, Gynecologic, and Neonatal Nursing* found that women typically experience dozens of interruptions during their first day after delivery. It found that from 8 a.m. until 8 p.m., new breastfeeding moms experienced 54 visits or phone calls, averaging seventeen minutes in length. They were alone with their babies (or the baby and the baby's father) only 24 times on average, and half of those episodes were nine minutes or less in duration.

These relentless interruptions make the flow of trying to learn a new skill, much less develop a relationship, nearly impossible. Often mothers feel too vulnerable while in the hospital to practice breastfeeding, with the likelihood of interruptions from either hospital staff or visitors.

If a baby is sleepy following a medicated birth, he may not fuss much over a few missed feedings, which can lead to an insufficient milk supply if this pattern is continued. This can be exacerbated by well-meaning but inaccurate advice to feed for short durations which is a very common but erroneous recommendation. (Wiessinger, West and Pitman, 2010)

Even if good information is provided during a mother and baby's hospital stay, it may be insufficient to get them off to a good start after they return home. Babies change dramatically in the early days, and information that was appropriate on day one may not be the right course of action later the same week. At an earlier point in human history, there would have been a greater consistency of support, a common knowledge of how breastfeeding works and needs to be supported. The group in which the woman and her baby lived, would have given them the tools and support to begin their life together. This is not the situation many new mother and babies find themselves following birth at the current moment in history.

Appropriate technology for birth.

In April 1985, the World Health Organization (WHO) and the Pan American Health Organization (PAHO) sponsored an interdisciplinary conference on appropriate technology for birth. A lengthy list of recommendations, reprinted in this article, was unanimously adopted by the conferees. Among the considerations addressed by the recommendations are a woman's right to exercise control over conditions of labor and delivery; the importance of communication between women, their families, and health personnel; and the need to make judicious use of technologies such as fetal monitoring. A network of evaluation groups to assess new technologies, sponsored by WHO and PAHO, is advocated. PIP: The European regional office of the World Health Organization (WHO), the Pan American Health Organization, and the WHO

regional office of the Americas held a conference in April on appropriate technology for birth. Held in Fortaleza, Brazil, the conference was attended by over 50 participants representing midwifery, obstetrics, pediatrics, epidemiology, sociology, psychology, economics, health administration, and mothers. Careful review of the knowledge of birth technology led to unanimous adoption of the recommendations which follow. WHO believes these recommendations to be relevant to perinatal services worldwide. Every woman has the right to proper prenatal care, and she has a central role in all aspects of this care, including participation in the planning, carrying out, and evaluation of the care. Social, emotional, and psychological factors are fundamental in understanding how to provide proper prenatal care. Although birth is a natural and normal process, even "no risk pregnancies" can result in complications. Sometimes intervention is necessary to obtain the best result. For the recommendations to be viable, a thorough transformation of the structure of health services is required together with modification of staff attitudes and the redistribution of human and physical resources. General recommendations include the following: health ministries should establish specific policies about appropriate birth technology for the private and nationalized health services; countries should carry out joint surveys to evaluate birth care technologies; and the whole community should be informed of the various procedures in birth care in order to enable each woman to choose the type of birth care she prefers. Specific recommendations include the following: The well-being of the new mother must be ensured through free access of a chosen member of her family during birth and throughout the postnatal period; women who give birth in an institution must retain their right to decide about clothing, food, disposal of the placenta, and other culturally significant practices; and the healthy newborn must remain with the mother whenever possible. The recommendations acknowledge differences between regions and countries. Implementation must be adapted to these special situations.

PMID: 2863457 [PubMed - indexed for MEDLINE]

v Lancet. 1985 Aug 24;2(8452):436-7.

Very little has changed since the WHO's Fortaleza Declaration except that intervention rates have skyrocketed without any dramatic improvement in perinatal and maternal mortality.

Compare the Fortaleza recommendations to your birth experience, those of your friends, or your experiences as a healthcare provider. "Standard" obstetric care is a series of managed rituals and stopwatches, not an evidence-based or woman-centered journey.

Here are the recommendations from the Fortaleza Declaration:

These 16 recommendations are based on the principle that each woman has a fundamental right to receive proper prenatal care:

That the woman has a central role in all aspects of this care, including participation in the planning, carrying out and evaluation of the care:

And those social, emotional and psychological factors are decisive in the understanding and implementation of proper prenatal care.

* The whole community should be informed about the various procedures in birth care, to enable each woman to choose the type of birth care she prefers.

* The training of professional midwives or birth attendants should be promoted. Care during normal pregnancy and birth and following birth should be the duty of this profession.

* Information about birth practices in hospitals (rates of cesarean sections, etc.) should be given to the public served by the hospitals.

There is no justification in any specific geographic region to have more than 10-15% cesarean section births (the current US c-section rate is estimated to be about 23%). [in 1985]

[Ed: The U.S. rate now is over 30%. The U.K., with a better developed but non-optimal midwifery system, has 23%; the Netherlands, 14%; Canada, 24%. In Chile, the overall rate is 40%, and the C section rate among women with private obstetricians there ranges from 57-83%, depending on the physician]

* There is no evidence that a cesarean section is required after a previous transverse low segment cesarean section birth. Vaginal deliveries after a cesarean should normally be encouraged wherever emergency surgical capacity is available.

* There is no evidence that routine electronic fetal monitoring during labor has a positive effect on the outcome of pregnancy.

* There is no indication for pubic shaving or a pre-delivery enema.

* Pregnant women should not be put in a lithotomy (flat on the back) position during labor or delivery. They should be encouraged to walk during labor and each woman must freely decide which position to adopt during delivery.

* The systematic use of episiotomy (incision to enlarge the vaginal opening) is not justified.

* Birth should not be induced (started artificially) for convenience and the induction of labor should be reserved for specific medical indications.

No geographic region should have rates of induced labor over 10%.

* During delivery, the routine administration of analgesic or anesthetic drugs, that are not specifically required to correct or prevent a complication in delivery, should be avoided.

* Artificial early rupture of the membranes, as a routine process, is not scientifically justified.

* The healthy newborn must remain with the mother whenever both their conditions permit it. No process of observation of the healthy newborn justifies a separation from the mother.

* The immediate beginning of breastfeeding should be promoted, even before the mother leaves the delivery room.

* Obstetric care services that have critical attitudes towards technology and that have adopted an attitude of respect for the emotional, psychological and social aspects of birth should be identified. Such services should be encouraged and the processes that have led them to their position must be

studied so that they can be used as models to foster similar attitudes in other centers and to influence obstetrical views nationwide.

* Governments should consider developing regulations to permit the use of new birth technology only after adequate evaluation.

Whether birthing in a hospital or at home, it is quite possible to have a birth that is satisfying, safe and biologically normal to you and your baby. I'd like to share the very different birth stories of my second and third children.

While making plans to have a home birth for my second child, I became very ill with a respiratory infection, which landed me in the hospital for a week at seven months into the pregnancy. My obstetrician was adamant that a home birth was no longer an option. By the end of my pregnancy I was much healthier, and even though I'd really wanted to give birth at home, I was resigned to birthing in the hospital.

As my due date approached and relatives arrived to help me with the older child, the familiar sensations began to let me know that the birth was not far off. While taking a walk with my dear mother-in-law, the Braxton-Hicks contractions were getting very close—two minutes apart—and my mother-in-law was getting quite worried that this was *it*. Since the contractions were virtually painless, I was pretty sure that they weren't terribly productive but decided to go to the hospital to get checked to prevent her from having a coronary event with worry.

The hospital check revealed what I'd already suspected—Braxton-Hicks, not quite to the finish line. After I was sent home we had a large, high carbohydrate dinner and went to bed, for a very short time. After getting adequate fuel, my body began kicking into real labor—back labor, unfortunately, but it was feeling quite productive this time. Not wishing to labor on my back, I elected to stay home and walked around the house, pausing with the more intense contractions and giving in to the progressing labor.

About eleven hours after labor had begun; it was getting clear that it was getting ready to peak. I woke up my husband, son, and in-laws, and we left in the early hours of dawn to return to the hospital. This time, as we arrived at the labor ward it was clear that we were going to bring a little one into the world in short order. The baby was a posterior presentation, which explained why the labor had been so intense. Within an hour of admission I was fully effaced, dilated to ten centimeters, and feeling that exquisite urge to push. A doctor was found who came and examined the situation and elected to hang around since a baby seemed imminent.

As the baby was starting to descend, he seemed to be stuck. As the physician -checked the reason for the hang-up it was revealed that the baby had the cord wrapped around his neck. His heart rate was getting lower, but not to the point of "must intervene" fetal distress. The doctor was calm, clear, and to the point: this little one needs to get out pretty quickly or we'll have to go in and get him.

My three-year-old had already seen his mommy taken away in an ambulance a couple of months earlier, and that hadn't gone too well. Subjecting him to another mother-being-carried-away event was not a good option. That was sufficient inspiration for me to take everything within and push the little guy out. He had the cord wrapped around his neck not once, but two times. He must have thought he needed to wear a tie to his birth.

His little purple body was taken to the table a few feet from me immediately after his birth for a few blow-by puffs of oxygen, and then back to me in just a few minutes. He rested on my chest and we all watched as his color quickly came back. Shortly afterward he started looking for something to eat and was soon nursing happily. I was basking in the afterglow of an unmedicated birth with endorphins coursing through my body.

It had been a difficult but empowering experience. My doctor had been fully supportive of my choices and clear about the issues of my baby's delivery, and we truly worked together to get him out and into the world. Having big brother come touch, kiss, and marvel over his new brother was worth all the effort at the very end. I can't imagine how much I'd have missed if I had been numbed and unable to fully participate in bringing my little Patrick into the warmth of his loving family.

When I found out I was pregnant with our third baby, I was delighted finally to be able to have a home birth. The pregnancy went well and there were no maternal illnesses to contend with this time. The baby was due in early December, around the time we have our annual Christmas party. For the first (and probably only) time in my life, everything was purchased and wrapped for Christmas. My husband joked that if I went into labor during the party he was going to sell tickets! A few days before the party, my bag of waters broke. I called my midwife and she said to keep her posted about when contractions began; they hadn't yet. There were a few Braxton-Hicks contractions during the day, but nothing that seemed very productive.

Later that evening I took the concoction of castor oil and orange juice that I was sure would get things going. My husband's business partner was celebrating his fortieth birthday at a party in his honor an hour away. I told my husband to go since the baby wouldn't arrive *that* quickly. Besides, my stepdaughter was staying with us with her five-week-old and we could handle things. After giving the boys their evening bath and getting them into bed with a story, the contractions began in earnest. By ten o'clock that night my husband, Jerry, had returned and the midwife was summoned.

During the pregnancy I'd had the opportunity to really get to know my midwife and her nurse as well. I knew that I would have her present at my birth and not someone I'd never met. That was something I had not experienced with my hospital births, although I'd been most fortunate to get two really great doctors by the luck of the draw.

When the midwife and her nurse arrived, they checked me out and we just chatted between contractions until they got too intense for conversation. When I didn't feel much like chatting, she was just "there" with me, allowing me to work through the contractions. At the point where I was reaching transition (the peak intensity of second stage labor), she suggested that I get into the tub and soak—we were fortunate enough to have a deep, Jacuzzi style tub. Experiencing transition under water was so very different from my other births. It was as if the pressure of the water on the outside of my body was canceling out the pressure from within, and before long I was ready to push. In retrospect it would have been easier just to finish in the tub, but I had bought new jammies for this birth and had to wear them! (Hooray for pregnant logic!)

Betsy, my step daughter, went to awaken the boys. The oldest, Paul, age six, had been practicing cutting balloons so he could cut the baby's umbilical cord. The pushing didn't last long. I was so comfortable in my own bed with my family close by. Soon the midwife, Leonette, told me to put my hand between my legs, and I felt my baby's head—hair! Jeanne came into the world a few minutes after midnight. Paul cut the cord like a champ. Baby was nursing within a short time, and we were all ready to cuddle up and get some sleep within a couple of hours of her birth.

It was a very empowering birth – only slightly over two hours of labor, and my little girl was nearly a pound heavier than her brothers were at birth. I felt as if I could do it again, easily, not the way I'd felt after my previous births at all. Even though I did experience some tearing during the delivery, it healed very quickly, especially compared to the episiotomy I had had with my first birth. All in all it was a great way to complete our family. Jeanne, now a young adult, has still never been in a hospital except as a visitor.

MOPPING UP THE MESS: STRATEGIES FOR A BETTER SOCIETY

BY MARGIE DEUTSCH LASH, MSED, IBCLC, RYT

One's philosophy is not best expressed in words; it's expressed in the choices one makes. In the long run, we shape our lives and we shape ourselves. The process never ends until we die. And then the choices we make are ultimately our responsibility.

—Eleanor Roosevelt

What Can We Do?

We have established that the highly technological society of today, with its innovations and instant solutions to all kinds of situations, makes for a complicated world into which we bring the most vulnerable members of our society—our children. These little people need the adults in their lives to understand how they develop and grow. They need us to advocate for them at all times, no matter what the cost to our way of life. We must make choices that support their optimal growth, choices that resonate with the world that they are experiencing. Their perceptions of the world really matter.

With all of these changes impacting us our most vulnerable members, our children, where has our society landed? What is it that we value? What practices support those values and would we keep? Where must we make course adjustments?

We Americans value egalitarianism and autonomy. Most of us see these as very good things. Yet, these good things can become harmful if taken to extremes. Might we be in danger of such extremes with our new technologies and loss of attachments to other human beings?

Society's Values and Meeting the Needs of Our Children

Our industrialized society has created a world in which it is increasingly difficult for us to stay focused on meeting the needs of our children. At every turn we are bombarded with visual depictions of advertisers telling us that we need this widget or that gadget. Historically, our industrialization has changed our society's goals from meeting individual needs to a deliberate focus on productivity. As a result of this change, our value system has changed as well so that now, in the technological age, we value the product over the process. Instead of enjoying the time we spend in the process, we are more concerned with the product we turn out. And yet, we as human beings are drawn to the process.

Let's look at one example of this emphasis on product versus process. Lots of cooking shows appear in the regular weekly television schedule. For example, one popular cooking program that airs several times each week deals with a challenge between two chefs. At the end of the competition the chefs are judged on their creations. The viewer witnesses the preparation of several courses of a meal. Points are given for creativity in the use of the ingredients, taste, and presentation. Forty-five minutes of the program are devoted to the process, the last fifteen minutes are devoted to the judging, and the winner of the competition is announced. The viewer has just spent his or her valuable time watching as the competitors painstakingly go through the process to create interesting courses using many different cooking strategies. If we were only interested in the outcome, why bother to watch the program? Why not just tune in to the last fifteen minutes and watch the results?

Interestingly, after watching the show I am often left a little disappointed. Three-quarters of the program shows the process, so the viewer would come to the logical conclusion that the process is what is important. However, the focus ends up being on the product. This is a pretty standard way in which our society deals with issues today.

Human beings are interested in the process it takes to arrive at a conclusion. We are drawn to the process involved in creating mouth-watering delicacies. Yet, the competition is judged solely on the outcome. Process is not even taken into consideration; no points are given for it. This is one example of a condition that is pervasive in our society today. We reward only the finished product.

There seems to be a major disconnect between process and product. On the one hand, we often evaluate outcomes by looking at productivity, i.e., how many cars can be manufactured per day, how many people can be seen by a doctor per day, how many children passed the English test today, how many people were served lunch today in the restaurant. For a moment let's look at other ways to focus our attention. For example, we might look at the quality of each car manufactured instead of the number of cars we can manufacture in one day. The patients seen by the doctor might be asked if they got their questions answered when they saw their doctor. We might look at what the children learned in English instead of how many passed the test. We might ask the people who were served lunch in the restaurant whether they enjoyed their meal and what suggestions they would have to improve the taste of the food.

It is not that one way of looking at a situation is better than another. We must take both parts of the situation—process and product—into account. In fact, I would even go as far as saying that process is more important in many ways than product, because it is the human element of any situation that makes life worth living. Part of our dilemma in modern times is the lack of interest on the part of society of putting emphasis on the process. The importance of relationships and our interactions must never be underestimated.

Let's look at another scenario in which we can focus on the process being more important than the finished product. In a learning environment we often have the opportunity to find such examples. Mathematics is a common subject where the act of finding an answer (the process) is as important as the product. Many students are frustrated by the fact that teachers often make the learners show the process of how they arrived at a particular answer. Teachers want to see the work so that they can determine whether the learner actually understands the concepts needed to arrive at a correct answer consistently. Students often say things like "as long as I got the right answer, why does showing my work matter?" The teachers are right in a sense. How we arrive at the answer is just as important as getting the correct answer. The process is important and it serves us well to look at it.

In an example like this, it serves us well to look at the process.

When we value the product more than the process that went into the making of that product, we devalue our time, energy, and interconnectedness to each other. We are a society built on human relationships. Yet every day most of us spend the majority of our time in industry. We focus our energies on being productive, instead of valuing the way we spend our day. How many times have you gotten to the end of your day and taken a moment to evaluate how your day was spent? What is your usual "answer"? Many of us say things like, "Oh, I didn't get anything accomplished today," or, "I wasted so much time today instead of being more productive." In the end, does it really matter that we didn't get our whole list of things completed? The reality is that we can just put those uncompleted tasks on our list for tomorrow. In most instances the completion of these tasks won't make a lot of difference in the overall big picture. The human relationships that we create are what matters. In the big picture, what we achieve each day from our task list doesn't matter nearly as much as the human relationships that we create. People don't reach the end of life and say things like, "I wish I had spent more time at work." However, many people realize too late that they didn't spend enough time with their family. In their early adult years they were busy working hard, spending many more hours away from the family than in the family's presence.

Taking time to "stop and smell the roses," pausing to answer our child's questions about the world and how it works, taking a few minutes to enjoy the sunset or the glow of the rising moon—these things matter. There are so many natural marvels all around us that we don't even see. Experiencing nature is a perfect way to come in contact with a slower way of life and an appreciation for the important elements of our lives. We can't rush the growth of a flower or, for that matter, the growth of a child. We can lose ourselves to the industry and production of our busy lives and in doing so, lose so very much more. The very essence of being human comes from the interactions that we have with those around us.

If, in fact, we lived in a world full of kind and compassionate human beings who related to each other in a totally harmonious manner then we wouldn't be having this conversation. Peace on Earth would be attainable in our lifetime. However, that is not the situation that we find ourselves in today. We live in a world full of intolerance for others. In politics, religion, and ethnicity we see people concentrating on the differences between people with much greater emphasis than on the similarities between people of different backgrounds, philosophies, and cultures.

Let's first concentrate our efforts on finding some of the common ground that we share before moving forward to try to right the wrongs of our society. Let's get in touch with our nurturing qualities and become true advocates for the children in our world. Each of us can make a difference. All it takes is dedication to the common goal of making our world a better place. That one basic value can take us a long way on our journey.

All around us we see a polarization of many aspects of life. For example, scientists and clergy often find that they are on different sides of issues having to do with research, medical procedures, and the definition of what constitutes life. We have a difficult time agreeing on what values are universal. We tend to find places of disagreement, rather than focusing on the common ground that exists between peoples and societies. Could we find ways to communicate that would breakdown these walls and barriers? I believe that humankind has the ability to listen to one another. Let's see if we can focus on the similarities between us, rather than the differences.

In the media today, we have begun to see an interest in evaluating our ideas about important elements of our society. For example, the British Broadcasting Corporation recently aired a news segment concerning public interest on the topic of having a job versus taking care of a family. People are beginning to ask questions about what really makes them feel fulfilled. Maybe society is ready for some bigger changes with respect to the choices we have made in the past.

Society's growing interest in caring for the world in a significant way is evidenced by a recent insert that appeared in many papers around the United States. The syndicated publication *Parade* magazine sponsored a contest entitled the *American Challenge to Better the World.* They published information on their challenge in the publication and gave Americans information on volunteering their time and making monetary contributions to a number of charitable organizations that could use help. The contest was to encourage people to visit the organizations' websites to become more involved. Ultimately, the non-profit organization that received the most "votes" would receive a monetary contribution from *Parade.* During the three weeks following the announcement of this challenge 50,000 people donated to 7,000 charities with contributions that totaled well over one million dollars.

Maybe society is ready to step up to the challenges that lay ahead. It's not going to be easy. We all need to roll up our sleeves and make a personal commitment to get involved in the process. Everyone can make a difference—one person at a time, one good deed at a time.

As you continue to read, you may want to keep paper and pencil nearby so that you can jot down your ideas as you think of them. We want you to come away from this book with a list of actions you are anxious to take in moving our society forward to a place that makes it possible for children to grow into independent, well-adjusted human beings.

I don't want to live in the modern world.
Lyrics by Billie Joe Armstrong from the song Modern World, Green Day,

— 21st Century Breakdown, April 2009

Living in the Modern World

Today's technology is at odds with the natural process of human development. As a student of child development theory, I have always had a problem with the way modern society has treated the mother-baby relationship. We can easily see all around us examples of ways for parents to avoid holding their babies. Pick up an issue of any parenting magazine and you will see a myriad of items designed to give the parents the ability to put their baby down. Having recently attended a baby shower, I was amazed at how industry continues to find additional products to hold and entertain an infant. It almost seems as if our economy, as if it has a mind of its own, is determined to keep our babies out of our arms.

The whole consumer society that we're imbedded in is really a system of delivering marvels. Toys, clothing, games, and entertainment: it's all to astonish and sweep you away.

—Terence McKenna, from John David Ebert's Twilight of the Clockwork God

We are told through the media—not just in advertising but also on the layette list provided in books, magazines, and at retail stores—that we need all of these things, that we can't possibly care for our babies unless we have all these wonderful, modern contraptions. We have strollers, cribs, car seats (a necessary piece of equipment that protects children from danger while riding in a car), rockers, and bouncy seats. However, these devices designed for the modern family fail to recognize the baby's unyielding need to be held and nurtured in his mother's arms as much as possible.

Do we really need all these things, or are many of these products simply undermining our ability to care for our children in the manner in which nature intended? I respectfully submit that so many of what we have come to accept as normal childrearing practices are anything but normal. It is not material and equipment that children need to grow and flourish, but closeness first to their mothers, and then fathers, and eventually to other family members and friends that encourages healthy emotional and physical growth.

A Historical Look at Family Structure

During the stone age, communities lived in groups that supported family units (Arts, 2008). It was essential for all members of the community to understand their responsibilities to the community and to work very hard to fulfill their commitments. Long gone are the days when extended families lived in the same community and saw each other on a daily basis. Long gone are the days when neighbors took care of each other. Today we live in nuclear families that often have very little support. Each family unit keeps much of their life private and feels it is inappropriate to "bother" others with their problems. Our society highly values this privacy and, in many cases, holds personal affairs "close to the vest," not allowing neighbors or extended family members to become involved in helping out with things like child care, shopping, and taking care of the sick. We have let our interest in privacy overshadow our need for help. This private independence creates distance in our relationships with others.

At the same time, technology keeps making strides that affect communication in a myriad of ways. Instead of walking to a neighbor's home, we might send him a text message. Instead of calling our extended family members, we might send them a message on a social networking website. Instead of talking to our family members over a meal, many families find themselves picking something up from a fast food restaurant drive-through and having their children eat in the car on the way to a lesson or sports practice. In days gone by, families almost always had a least one daily meal together, uninterrupted by television or telephone calls. Meal time was often the central meeting time for families to touch base and communicate about what was going on in their lives. Quality time was easy to find because everyone in the family valued the time they spent together. It was a normal and natural part of life. The way we live today is very unlike those earlier times.

Today, much of the time that the family spends together is spent in structured events instead of unstructured time to just "hang out" and be present in one another's lives. This doesn't allow family member to interact with each other in ways that have always defined and unified the family unit in the past. Yet for many families the kinds of structured activities in which they engage are the only things they do together as a family. Many people feel unfulfilled with this kind of interaction and long for a deeper, more significant way to interact.

Our family structures have changed a great deal over the millennia. Instead of living in close-knit communities, many families are separated geographically from their extended families and do not have the kinds of resources once available in smaller community groups. This lack of community has made it even more difficult for families to be able to function in a healthy manner. The isolation that many families feel is palpable. It is more the exception than the rule that people simply wave hello to their neighbors from afar. They might not even have their neighbors' phone numbers or know their names.

The Benefits of Building a Community

We must find a balance in our busy lives while focusing on the societal values that will enable us to be the kind of parents we need to be. In order to raise children who will be able to function in the society of tomorrow, we must provide them with an environment that is full of love and support. We must find the very best means of helping our children strive to be compassionate human beings who live each and every day with the intention to do what is best for all humankind. This is the task at hand.

One way of creating this kind of situation would be building supportive communities of like-minded people. We would be better able to meet the needs of our children with a supportive group of people who are committed to a set of common values. In joining together with others we may find the kind of psychological support that we all need to grow as a society and to meet our optimal potential.

The joy of living in community with others includes having a support system that can be easily activated in times of need. We could all benefit by allowing others to be involved in our daily lives in the ways listed in the previous section about family structure. Instead of reinventing the wheel, we could take a lesson from the past. We need only to open ourselves up to the possibilities of taking part in this kind of community.

In order to make the changes that this kind of community would require, people need to be willing to let go of some degree of their privacy. Building a community based on the basic human values of love and support for others is an important first step.

Societal Support of Families

We must take a look at our values when determining how best to support families. As a society we need to pinpoint some core values that we can agree are important. Here is a list of ideas:

- Acceptance: Learn to accept that which allows for individual differences and work together to resolve issues that affect the normal growth and development of our most vulnerable citizens—our children
- Communication: Effectively conveying our thoughts and beliefs is one of the most important elements of every relationship
- Respect: Demonstrate respect for yourself and for others

- Mindfulness: Live each day with an awareness concerning your actions
- Intention: Set an intention for each of your activities—think about what drives your decision-making

Recently I received an email with pictures of people from around the world and the foods they ate on a weekly basis. I immediately noticed that the poorer the population, the happier they actually looked. It appeared that the people who were able to provide for their own sustenance had a glow that people who were pictured with processed packaged foods did not have. This made me stop and think about the way we live in the developed world. We are often caught up in the material world around us. We sometimes think that having more will make us happy, and yet it seems that money can't buy happiness. I know it is a cliché. However, it is so very true.

Most socioeconomic groups are struggling more today than they were several years ago. Groups that had disposal income are finding that they no longer have a financial cushion. People that were already struggling are finding it very difficult to make ends meet. The kinds of action items listed at the end of this section will help you to see how the economy is not important to making the kinds of changes that we need to improve our way of life. It isn't economic wealth that we are seeking. It is the deeper satisfaction that comes from close family ties and strong friendships. The bottom line is that interpersonal relationships are what really form the structure for happiness in life.

Birth Practices: Do they have an effect on children's growth and development?

Birth practices in our culture are a prime example of the way our society needs to change in order to achieve the human connectedness we so long for. Let's take a look at birthing trends today.

Many would agree that we began moving away from the needs of the mother and baby and into the realm of a medicalized birth when childbirth moved from the home to the hospital by the middle of the twentieth century. Previously, birth was not considered a medical procedure or condition but as normal and natural, an event for which women needed the assistance of a support person knowledgeable in the process of birth. Usually, this support person was a midwife. The midwife was specially trained (most often through an apprenticeship) to assist women in childbirth. Prenatal care was done by the midwife. Pregnancy was considered a natural time in the woman's life. We did not see birth as something that required medical intervention.

Today statistics indicate that experienced midwives have outcomes as good as doctor-assisted births (Janssen, February 5, 2002). Over the past several decades we have seen a renewed interest in birthing women being attended by midwives and doulas (birth assistants). This has given rise to a whole new model for birthing practices in the developed world. Often developing countries are much more supportive of women during their stage of childbirth. When birthing women are empowered to advocate for themselves and their babies, infant and maternal morbidity and mortality rates are much lower. When the power is taken away from women through the medical system, both infant and maternal morbidity and mortality rates increase (Martin, 2009). Historically, hospitals have been places to go when one is sick, so going to the hospital to birth a baby brings fear of the unknown for many women as they anticipate medical interventions in which they may or may not be willing participants.

The medical establishment need not feel threatened by the power of the women in their care. On the contrary, they should feel gratified that women want to be actively involved in their births. This dynamic creates the opportunity for a team approach between mother-to-be, father-to-be, doctor, nurses, midwife and doula (labor support person) with the birthing woman being an integral part of the team.

When women feel empowered and take an active role in their birth process they make it possible to achieve the birth of their choice. No longer do they fall prey to those around them that may be suggesting less than optimal birth interventions. They become their own advocates. They are able to stand up for themselves and can direct how others are able to help them. They are put in the driver's seat instead of needing to rely on those around them to tell them what to do. This empowerment will occur when women feel supported in their choices about birth and they have access to all the information that will help them to feel the power that their bodies have in the birthing process. We need to be sure that women are informed about their birth choices and educated about the physical process that takes place as they birth their babies. With women taking their part in the birth process seriously better outcomes will likely result.

Women need to feel comfortable in their birthing environment. When they feel comfortable in their setting they can relax and concentrate on the process that is taking place in their bodies. They have the ability to stay focused on the moment without being distracted by what is going on around them. Without fear they will remain confident and powerful thus, allowing a more peaceful satisfying birth—a birth in which they will be proud. Instead of feeling like a victim of the situation they are completely involved in the process.

"The moment a child is born, the mother is also born. She never existed before. The woman existed, but the mother, never. A mother is something absolutely new."

—Bhagwan Shree Rajneesh

For some women childbirth may be their first opportunity to take control of their world in such an empowering manner. The power of being in control of the situation may have long-reaching effects in other areas of her life. I have seen women come alive in a different way because of the empowerment they have felt in childbirth. Certainly, the moment that I became a mother had an almost hypnotic effect on me. I knew at that moment that I was a changed forever. I would always be a mother from that day forward. Nothing could ever change that fact. I felt that it was a magical moment.

When birth took place at home, babies came when they were ready. Labor would begin spontaneously signaling that her baby was ready to be born. Forty weeks gestation was considered a guideline, the average number of weeks that a woman would be pregnant, not an absolute time to give birth.

The intricate dance that begins even before birth between the mother and baby is an indication of the complexity and interrelation of this all important relationship.

In fact, the fetus signals the mother that he is ready for the birth process to begin when his lungs reach a maturational point that will allow him to live outside his mother's body. When this point is reached the fetus releases chemicals into the maternal blood stream that signal the process to begin (Mendelson, July 2009). If labor is induced through the use of drugs this delicate, natural process is upset.

It is interesting to note that with the medicalized birth system of today, our infant mortality rate is very high, when compared with other countries. The most current statistics available from the Centers for Disease Control at the time of this writing were for 2004. The United States ranked 29th in infant mortality in a three-way tie with Poland and Slovakia. Nearly seven U.S. babies die out of every 1,000 live births. The top three spots in infant mortality are held by the Asian countries of Singapore, Hong Kong, and Japan. The next three spots are held by the Scandinavian countries of Sweden, Norway, and Finland. All of these countries achieve 2 to 3.3 deaths in 1,000 live births. (National Vital Statistics, 2008)

Birth practices in the countries that have achieved better infant mortality rates are often more mother-centered. In those countries women have achieved a level of autonomy concerning birth options that allow natural birth assisted by midwives and with few medical interventions. Women are encouraged to make decisions regarding their pregnancy and the manner in which they birth their babies. This empowerment of women is not just a nice extra, as stated in the citation listed here. (Wagner, Issue 75, Autumn 2005) It is an essential element of life that makes society strong. The wonderful side effect of this empowerment of women is that birth outcomes are much improved. Thus we see much lower infant mortality rates.

Of course, we must acknowledge that our medical care has helped women hold on to pregnancies that would otherwise miscarry, and has helped families that have had difficulty becoming pregnant to have children. Technology has allowed us to achieve some dramatic and awesome outcomes. We even have several medical specialties that have come out of the technological advances in obstetrical care—that of perinatologist and neonatologist. These two specialties, respectively, deal with high-risk pregnancies (i.e. advanced maternal age, gestational diabetes, and pregnancy-induced hypertension,) and newborns with special needs (i.e. preterm infants, congenital anomalies, and infants that have birth trauma issues). These special situations fall outside the normal, full term births that the majority of women will have.

The medical establishment need not feel threatened by the power of the women in their care. On the contrary, they should feel gratified that women want to be actively involved in their births. Women must feel empowered and take an active role in their birth process. We need to be sure that women are informed about their birth choices and educated about the physical process that takes place as they birth their babies. As women take their part in the birth process seriously, better outcomes likely will result. Women need to feel comfortable in their birthing environment so that they can feel relaxed and in control of their situation.

Looking at Birth Today

Today many women have induced labors. The reasons for a labor induction can vary from the convenience of being able to plan when the birth will occur, to being past full gestation (over 40 weeks), to maternal or fetal issues that can be very serious. Some inductions are absolutely necessary. However, induced labor for the sake of convenience should be carefully evaluated. This practice is not best for the baby (Caughey AB, 2009 Mar).

Recently I was speaking to a woman who had almost reached her due date. She was sharing that at her last appointment her obstetrician had asked her if she wanted to be induced. She looked at him in disbelief. She said to me, "Why would I want to be induced before my due date?" Then her doctor said to her how long past her due date was she willing to go before an induction. She felt that as long as everything was going well, she wanted to wait for the baby to signal when he was ready for his birth. In other words, she wanted to let a spontaneous labor occur with no help from medical intervention.

Unfortunately, her response is not the default position. Many women do not ask for an explanation about why a doctor is recommending an induction. Women often place their trust in their healthcare provider without question.

Maybe we need to rethink this. Education is the key. To be empowered to give birth with confidence is a process that requires information being shared with women during their pregnancy. The more educated a woman is about the process of birth, the more involved she can be in the experience. Knowledge is power. All women deserve to have the knowledge to come to birth with confidence. Childbirth education must include a comprehensive array of ideas and choices that women can internalize and accept as their very own.

Of course, we have all kinds of technology today that can benefit both moms and babies. By using these technologies in combination with a reasonable approach to birth and educated, informed mothers, we can find a happy balance in which families have access to a birth situation that is both rewarding and safe.

As birth practices became more medicalized, technology marched forward without regard to the manner in which children develop. Technologies and drugs, often developed to assist a high-risk couplet, instead became used for every pair and prevented the natural process from unfolding. This is often inappropriate. Not every laboring woman needs an IV, not every woman needs an epidural, and not every woman needs an episiotomy. All of these interventions have their place. In a normal, vaginal birth many of the interventions are not necessary or even advisable. Sadly, they are often recommended or even done without the mother's consent.

Each of these interventions has its place, but in a normal, vaginal birth many of the interventions are not necessary or even recommended.

Nurses often find themselves obligated to manage the technologies, rather than minister to the patients. Lawsuits and fear have created defensiveness in medical practice and a relationship of adversarial suspicion between providers and patients.

Before birth was moved into the hospital setting, mothers and babies stayed together after birth, not routinely separated. Attachment and bonding happened in a natural manner, without any special care. As we mentioned in the first section, attachment is paramount to healthy growth and development of the child. Without a secure attachment from birth, normal development is much more difficult. We must support a healthy attachment in all of our interactions with moms and babies.

Since the middle of the twentieth century, when hospital birth became the norm, we have seen many changes in the way mothers and babies receive postpartum care. Until recently mothers and babies were routinely separated at hospital births for a period of time. This separation began the downward spiral of problems associated with modern birthing practices, which often make attachment much more difficult. Research supports mothers and babies being given the opportunity to remain together for the first several hours after birth.

The cascade of interventions that might occur during childbirth can set up many barriers for the mother-baby pair that makes the establishment of their attachment much more difficult. Below is a list of these practices that very often have a negative impact on the mother-baby relationship:

- **Induced labor**

  Birth is generally a natural process that occurs when the fetus signals the mother's body to go into labor. When this process is artificially induced through the use of medications, manipulation, or even natural remedies, the mother-baby pair is put at higher risk for birth complications.

- **Routine recommendation of anesthesia**

  Women who choose hospital births are often misled by their health care providers to expect that anesthesia is necessary. It is important to point out that anesthesia can be harmful and does have risks. (Eberle RL, 1996) When women are empowered to give birth, they often are not in need of anesthesia. Knowledge of what actually occurs in the woman's body during the birth process can assist a woman in making the best choices for her and her yet-unborn child. As long as labor is progressing in a normal fashion, there is no need for anesthesia. Often it is the fear of the unknown that draws a woman to request anesthesia, or a caregiver to recommend that maybe a woman has reached the point where she no longer can tolerate the pain. It would be helpful for labor support people to point out to the mother that when she feels that the pain is almost unbearable she is probably in transition and that labor is probably nearing an end. It is lack of knowledge that leads so many women to thinking that they need anesthesia for childbirth.

- **Vacuum extraction/Forceps**

  If the mother is not able to push the infant out, vacuum extraction may be used to assist. This can cause bruising of the infant's head, and in turn the bruising may add to the incidence of newborn jaundice. This condition often causes an infant to be lethargic and not to feed well. Sometimes this procedure is the result of anesthesia given to the mother during labor. If she has had epidural or spinal anesthesia, she may not have the urge to push the baby out or she may not be physically able to push because of numbness in her pelvic region, making vacuum extraction much more likely.

In extreme cases, forceps are sometimes necessary to literally pull the infant out. Since the advent of vacuum extraction this practice is used much less often than it had been in the past. The birth literature has documented many examples of poor birth outcomes from forceps use. Placing the device on the infant's delicate, soft tissue is a difficult process that must be undertaken with the utmost care.

- **Cesarean birth**

The percentage of primary Cesarean births (first-time surgical births) in the United States is very high compared to many other developed countries. In our society today we often find that obstetrical care relies on Cesarean birth as a standard procedure, and we do not consider surgical birth to be unusual or out of the ordinary. This is in opposition to countries like Sweden where surgical births are much less common. We also find family-friendly governmental support in Sweden. Might there be some correlation? In the 1990s Sweden had a Caesarian birth rate of about 10.84[6] compared to the United States rate of 22.7 for the same year. (In 2003 the United States rate for Caesarian birth had risen to 27.5.)[7] Sweden has a long history of encouraging midwife-assisted home birth. This birthing option empowers and supports mothers by framing birth as a process in which the birthing woman is in charge of her birth, and she is assisted by her birth team that may include a labor coach (doula) and midwife or doctor. Societies in which women are empowered in the birthing process and are supported in their mothering often have statistically lower Caesarian birth rates. This is an interesting observation.

- **Mother-infant separation after birth**

Many communities today are seeing a change in the routine separation of mothers and infants after birth. Research has

---

6 (Nielsen, Olausson, & Ingemarsson, April 2, 2007)
7 (Menacker, September 22, 2005)

shown that keeping mothers and infants together for a period of at least two hours after birth facilitates all kinds of positive outcomes including, but not limited to, appropriate bonding and easier initiation of breastfeeding.[8] In the past, hospitals routinely separated mothers and infants very soon after birth, moving infants to a nursery where centralized nursing care was delivered. At the same time mothers were cared for by different nurses who didn't have anything to do with the care of the infants. Over the past ten or fifteen years, as research has become more and more clear on this topic, couplet care delivered by a single nurse is becoming the standard of care. The advantages of both mother and infant being cared for by the same nurse include appropriate attention to feeding cues of the baby, with one nurse responsible to see that mother and baby are supported and assisted in the optimal manner. Couplet care is defined as care given to mother and infant by the same nurse at the same time. Rooming-in (the term used to describe infants staying with their mothers in the same room) is also becoming the standard of care. This, too, facilitates bonding and attachment while allowing the mother to get to know her baby with the safety net of the nurse available for guidance and assistance if necessary.

During the second half of the twentieth century, babies were handled by others for weighing, measuring, and washing before being handed to mom as a swaddled bundle. Many studies on maternal-infant attachment clearly demonstrate that even a short separation may cause ongoing damage to this all-important bond between mother and child.[9] Current research has also identified several potential problems with the once again renewed practice of swaddling.[10] When babies are wrapped tightly in a blanket they do not have the freedom of movement that is best for their physical development. They are also deprived of the touch of their mother's skin. Lacking

8 (Bergman, Linley, & Fawcus, June 2004; Bergman, Linley, & Fawcus, June 2004)
9 (Mogi, Nagsawa, & Kikusui, September 9, 2010)
10 (Van Sleuwen, MSc, Boere-Boonekamp, Kuis, Schulpen, & L'Hoir, October 2007)

the sensory experiences intended to give the infant the ability to continue on his developmental journey, and from which he learns about the world around him, can be very detrimental to his physical health and emotional well-being. Infants require physical touch from those close to them so that they can attach appropriately and build the skills to interact in a healthy way with those who love and care for them. Infant development depends on significant skin-to-skin contact with the primary caregiver, the mother.

Both mother and child need to have uninterrupted contact so that they can form the physical and emotional attachment that will create an ongoing relationship that is integral to the infant's life. The primary attachment of an infant needs to be with his mother or the person that assumes the mother role. Through the relationship between infant and caregiver, the child learns basic coping skills, develops relationships, and forms fundamental personality characteristics. The mother/caregiver provides a relationship of safety and security that the child can depend upon. The process of attachment between the mother and child provides a mutual regulatory system which has an influence on the way mother and child interact with each other. After a period of months (different amounts of time for each child because development happens on a continuum that varies according to societal, psychological, and environmental factors) the child is ready to move to important secondary relationships which include other family members (most notably his father). Because the length of time needed varies from child to child, it needs to unfold as a natural process for each infant. The infant needs to determine when the time is right.

What the mother and infant really need is to be left alone to continue the process that began before birth—that is, the all-important, delicate dance of attachment, mother to infant and infant to mother. This process begun during pregnancy should not be interrupted. We must as a society support this mother-child bonding by providing an environment that facilitates continuing bonding and attachment from the first moments of life outside the womb, whether that birth takes place in a hospital, birth center, or home.

- **Brain Development: What actually happens**

At birth, the infant is a totally sensory being. He experiences the world through his five senses—taste, smell, touch, sight, and hearing. So when he needs something he will communicate with us through non-verbal cues at first. If we don't respond to his needs, he will revert to crying because that is the only means he has to clearly communicate his needs to us in the early weeks of life. For example, when a young infant is hungry he will smack his lips, turn his head side to side, and move his arms and legs to get our attention. If we don't respond to these early hunger cues, he will begin crying to be sure that we respond to his need.

All of his needs create appropriate sensory sensations in his body that are experienced as either positive or negative sensations. As a result, his behavior is solely related to these sensory impressions. If he feels good (positive sensation), he might coo or smile. If he feels uncomfortable (a negative sensation), he might fuss or cry. All his experiences in the early weeks and months can be categorized as positive or negative from a sensory perspective. We see this through his behavior.

The young infant is able to relate to life only on a sensory level because that part of his brain is functioning at birth. Sensory experiences are a result of activity in the right hemisphere of the brain. The right hemisphere is active and functions at a very high level from birth. The right side of the brain is much more mature than the left side of the brain at birth. Cognitive function that accounts for our ability to think and reason emanates from the left hemisphere of the brain. So when we look at child development we must be aware of how the process unfolds. Over the first three years of life a child moves through the sensory-motor stage of development. As the child grows and matures, the left hemisphere of his brain begins to develop with synapses (brain connections) being built that will allow him to respond to his experiences with greater maturity. Ultimately he will develop the ability to communicate with language, and a greater range of skills will be at his fingertips as he is able to physically manipulate objects and engage in more and more difficult thought processes. These are all signs that the left hemisphere of his brain is developing as it should.

In looking at brain development, it is interesting to draw on Jill Bolte Taylor's description of what happens to a person who suffers a brain trauma. In her book *My Stroke of Insight,* she points out that when an adult experiences an insult or trauma to the left hemisphere of the brain, the person very often reverts to infantile kinds of behavior. Often stroke victims who have had trauma to the left hemisphere of their brains become much more in touch with their senses. Sometimes they have difficulty speaking or cannot speak at all. They live in their bodies without the ability to engage in verbal communication. Taylor describes her recovery from this kind of brain trauma as a kind of starting over. She describes the feelings that she experienced after her stroke as a kind of drawing in and feeling good about being in this state. The right hemisphere of her brain was intact and functioning normally. Because of her work as a brain anatomist before her stroke she knew a great deal about the inner brain functioning. When she experienced her brain trauma, she was able to follow her experience from beginning to end from a place of great knowledge about the brain and later to describe it in detail.

Her description can be applied to the normal process of how infants mature in their development, from the highly functioning right hemisphere (where all sensory information is processed) at birth to a more mature left hemisphere (where cognitive abilities reside). As the synapses in the left hemisphere of the brain develop, the child begins to use cognitive skills. He learns to communicate through language and the full range of cognitive abilities that will serve him in his adult life when he reaches full maturation.

According to the famous child developmental specialist Jean Piaget, full cognitive function occurs in humans around adolescence. Until then children are not capable of responding to the world in an adult manner. However, we often expect children to act like adults as soon as they are able to communicate well. In fact, we often treat young children as if they are little adults. We expect them to sit still at a desk in a classroom for several hours. We expect them to listen to others speak without interrupting. These are not appropriate expectations for young children, and our teaching methods are often based on these inappropriate expectations. Do we want to develop a community of learners that can think independently and creatively? If so, the methods we use to educate our children need to include interactive, action-oriented experiences that will fascinate, inspire, and motivate them. (See the chapter entitled *Learning Environments/ Education*.)

At birth the left hemisphere is immature. Synapses will develop over the next few months that will account for the developmental milestones that we witness in the infant as he grows and matures. Synapses continue to develop over the course of childhood and into maturity. This is the process that enables us to continue to build our body of knowledge over many years. Not until old age do we begin to have a deterioration of those brain connections.

An understanding of the manner in which the brain develops from infancy to maturity helps us to put into perspective the importance of nurturing and supporting this all-important time in a person's life. To ensure healthy child development we must support and encourage appropriate attachment between mother and child.

Parenting Strategies

Who ever said that it would be easy being a parent?

In fact, it is the most difficult job of all. So much is riding on our skills to be the best parents we can be. Future generations are counting on us to know how to be good parents and to use our skills to create an environment where our children will grow up to be valued members of society, who will add their contributions to the world in countless ways. We must take this responsibility very seriously.

A Brief Historical Perspective on Parenting

The depression made an indelible impression on the youth that came of age during this difficult time in our history. World War II changed the face of the world by giving rise to industry unknown in previous times. The energy of the time called for growth in urban living and a spirit that collectively gave rise to unprecedented growth in automation as women entered the workforce in record numbers. The consciousness of the time seemed to center on an effort to grow into a society that was based on capitalism and the "American Dream" to be financially successful.

The extended family living and growing up in the same neighborhood began to fall away. The concept of the nuclear family (a mother, father, and their children), where support from the extended family was no longer available in many cases, became the rule rather than the exception. Many people moved to cities and learned a new way of being productive. Work became the centerpiece of many peoples' lives. Time for leisure activities began to erode.

During the 1950s child development theorists like Jean Piaget were finding new ways to think about children. Academics began to understand that children were not just little adults. We realized that the process of human development takes time and at birth the human brain is fully functioning, not the blank slate it was once thought to be.

Many years passed before the information we have today about child development was available to a wide audience. Parents who were brought up during the depression and World War II wanted their children to able to make an income that would support their families. In large part, they were concerned about their children learning a skill and getting an education that would allow the children to better their position in the world by making enough money in an industry that would give them some degree of security.

The children born in the years following World War II are referred to as Baby Boomers. They grew up in a time of unprecedented riches and growth of industry. We are now seeing the results of the parenting choices of those children, whose focus was to provide a gentle environment in which their children could grow and thrive. The Boomers wanted their children to have more than they had as they grew up. The promise of a life even better than when they grew up was foremost in their thinking. They were concerned with raising children with good self-esteem. Their focus was not how much money the children would make, but how happy they would be.

Commercial influences added a dimension to the growth of these children of the Baby Boomers, who were brought up around all kinds of electronic marvels. New and innovative television programming that included fast-paced, rapidly flashing screens changed the kinds of stimulation and dynamics to which children and adolescents were exposed (e.g., music videos, video games). The use of MP3 players and personal DVD players has enabled young people to tune in to their music or DVD while they disconnect from human interaction. It is so easy for people to keep their earphones plugged in while they travel to school or work. Instead of talking to their friends or family members, they can stay in their own world through shutting out normal communication with others.

On a recent air travel trip across the United States, I watched a mother and her young child interact. Her son, around four years old, was animated and pleasant during the first part of the trip. The mother had planned ahead and brought all kinds of activities for her son to keep him entertained and busy during the flight. She was wonderful in her interactions with him and he, in turn, responded to her with respect and age-appropriate comments. About midway through the flight the mom turned on a DVD for her son. This seemingly simple and benign event started a downward spiral that caused this little boy to pull his focus directly into the technology and away from those around him. He disengaged totally from his interactions with his mom. He sat quietly during the rest of the flight and watched the movie. When the flight attendant announced that it was time to turn off all personal electronic devices to prepare for landing, the little boy started fussing and feuding with his mom. It was a very dramatic change from his previous pleasant behavior during the time of their interactions during the beginning of the flight. The mother was so in tune with her son that she didn't make a big deal out of his fussing. She did not try to reason with him. Instead, she waited for the flight attendant to come by their row.

Quietly, she asked the flight attendant to explain to her son that it was time to turn off the DVD player. The flight attendant was very happy to speak to the little boy. She explained in simple language that it was necessary for him to turn off the DVD player because we needed to prepare for the pilot to safely land the plane. The mother was able to avoid conflict by simply allowing the little boy to hear the news from someone that he saw as an authority figure—someone in uniform that he knew had his best interests at heart.

There was no way this mom was going to be able to reason with her son. He just is not developmentally at a stage where reason is a possibility. It occurred to me that the change in this little boy's behavior seemed to be a result of his being glued to the technology (he was emotionally disengaged). He was not interacting with his mom for over an hour. This is a common response of young children to separation from their family members. In this particular case the mother and child were not physically separated. They were simply separated by the technology that drew his attention away from his interaction with his mother to a much more passive focus on watching the DVD.

In our culture we call people who sit watching television "couch potatoes," meaning that these people are as active as a potato. Potatoes don't take action. They are inanimate objects that have no ability to interact with their environment and the people in it. This seems to be a common problem when children, in particular, tune out of the relationships they have with others. Participating in a passive, non-action-oriented endeavor over a period of time makes it difficult to disengage and to begin to relate to others. For example, think about how wrapped up you get when you sit at your computer. When we turn on the computer to check email or search for information about something on the internet, many of us enter a trance-like state. We get engrossed in the activity at hand and tune many other things out. Somehow we tend to exclude others when we tune in to the technology. Have you ever been talking to someone and known that you didn't have their full attention? I would venture to say that in most cases it is because the person you are talking to is trying to do something technology related while you are talking to them (e.g., texting a friend on their cell phone, checking their email, or playing a game on a personal electronic device.)

Today communication happens in a very different manner than when the Baby Boomers were growing up. Today's generation of parents use instant messaging on the computer and text messaging from their cell phones to interact with each other. They are likely to have accounts on social networking sites such as MySpace and Facebook, where they can interact with hundreds of people every day. They can have global relationships where communication happens at the press of a button or a click of the mouse. The sharing of information can be immediate, compared to the communication of the past generations that required writing letters, making phone calls, going to libraries, and researching in books. Today parents have the internet at their fingertips. They can find information on virtually any subject in a matter of seconds. How often do you hear someone say, "Let's go check that out on the internet"?

However, the ability to critically evaluate the information we receive is often not taken into account. If we see it on the screen, we tend to believe it. It used to be that we had to teach people to critically analyze what they read in newspapers. Now we need to make sure that we use those same critical thinking skills to evaluate the information we find on the internet.

Parents of the Next Generation

As children, the parents of the current and next generations grew up in an unprecedented period of time when technological innovations exploded. Products were designed to attract their attention in ways never before imagined. Previously called the MTV generation or the Me generation, they identify with quick-moving, fast-paced communication styles. Often referred to as Generation X (birth dates1965-1980) and Generation Y (or Millenials) (birth dates 1981-1995), these young adults will be raising the next generation of children in ways very different from the way Baby Boomers were raised.

These young adults are the children of the Baby Boomer generation who were concerned to a high degree about raising children with good self-esteem and a joy for life. The Baby Boomers were raised by parents who grew up during the depression and had a strong work ethic pounded into their heads by parents who were determined to have their children be more successful than they were.

The Gen X and Y parents have their priorities clearly delineated, with friends and family relationships high on their list of importance. Their idea of a good job might have more to do with the kind of work they do than the amount of money they make.

Today we are more likely to come in contact with people that don't read the newspaper, but get their news on the internet, often as breaking news is actually occurring. Very often people of the Gen X and Y generations have little patience to wait for anything. They want what they want—and they want it now. Parenting requires lots of patience. Children develop on a much slower continuum than the parents may be willing to accept. Gen X and Y parents want a quick fix for the problems they encounter. For example, a new mother who is having trouble getting her baby to breast is happy to accept a device that will help her or she is happy to pump milk for her baby. We have an interesting dynamic that to date is unprecedented. Women are actually choosing to "breast milk feed" their babies (pumping their milk and giving that pumped milk to their baby in bottles) rather than breastfeeding them actually at the breast. These Gen Xers and Yers feel that is something that they can do more easily. If they are presented with a problem, they want to find a solution as quickly as possible, even if that means the solution is much less desirable than the original goal (which, in this example, was breastfeeding).

We now have research-based evidence that breastfeeding is much more than a feeding method. Breastfeeding allows mother and child to bond in the most appropriate manner. Breastfeeding provides a secure place for a child to get all of his needs met—nutritional, emotional, and social. Maybe the young-adults of today need to take a moment to reevaluate their choices. The easiest solution may very well not be the solution that is in the best interest of the children in our care.

What is the purpose of a child's cry?

Does a child cry to make us angry or anxious or disturb our peace and quiet? In the early months of a child's life crying is a major means of communication. Most babies rarely cry once their parents recognize their needs and respond appropriately. Crying is often the result of parents who have missed their baby's earlier cues. With respect to feeding behaviors, an infant's earlier cues include the simple act of waking, moving his limbs, turning his head side to side, smacking his lips. And yet, in the early weeks parents are often unaware that these behaviors are clear signals to the mother that it is time to feed the baby. Parents wonder how they will ever recognize these non-verbal cues, but most parents are able to recognize them by the time their infant reaches the age of two or three months.

However, if parents are not aware of the fact that babies communicate in many non-verbal ways and that crying is a very late cue that the baby is in need of attention, a baby may learn to use crying as his primary way to communicate. When an infant is picked up within ninety seconds from the onset of crying, cortisol release stops. The research done on this topic is clear and significant. This action signals the body that the stressful situation has come to an end and the baby will begin to "come down." (Thoman, 1975) From a developmental point of view, a child is free to grow to the next stage when parents stay in touch with him. In fact, the more connected a mother is to her child, the sooner she will be able to recognize these communication behaviors. If a mother is separated from her baby for even short periods of time in the early months, she will have a much more difficult time recognizing these cues that make life with baby such a pleasure.

In my work with families since the 1970's an ever-present question that new parents ask is, "How do we know what our baby needs?" This is a universal concern of mothers. Often, when I see these families again, they are confidently meeting their child's needs without even thinking about it. In normal, healthy environments the attachment process happens naturally. This is not something that we need to manufacture. Parents have the innate ability to discover the non-verbal communication cues that allow their child to grow and develop in a healthy manner. All parents can benefit from acquiring some knowledge about child development so that they can respond appropriately to these cues.

As healthcare professionals who specialize in maternal-child care, my colleagues and I always tell parents that their baby will teach them what they need to know to care for him or her. We just need to listen. Learning to "read" a child's behavior is a process that comes as the parent stays in tune with her child.

How Should We Respond to a Child's Cry?

Here is an example of one mother's account of how she was able to get her son to sleep through the night. See what you think of her method. One mother recently described to me how she had to leave her home so that she didn't have to hear her baby cry. The first night dad reported that the baby cried for 3 hours. The second night he cried for about 2-1/2 hours and on the third night the baby didn't cry for his mother any longer. This mother reported that this method was a complete success. Was this really an accomplishment? What had this technique achieved?

The baby learned that he could not trust his parents to meet his need for comfort, love and security. The mother became a bit more disconnected in her relationship with her child. She also "learned" that her intuition to listen to her baby's cry by comforting him was incorrect.

So, the question again—did this method of parenting work for the mother and child? The answer is a resounding "no". The mother may have gotten the superficial result she was looking for (in this case, a child who sleeps through the night), but to what end? The attachment between mother and child has been seriously disrupted causing trauma for the short-term for both mother and child. More importantly, though, this parenting strategy may cause lasting damage to the child later, manifesting as anywhere from minor to serious psychological difficulties.

When parents are able to meet their child's needs, the child has the ability to grow to the next developmental stage with no difficulty. Conversely, when we ignore their needs we create a situation that does not allow us to communicate with our children. It is our job as parents and child advocates to always keep the lines of communication with our children open and flowing in both directions.

Society often takes the position that we need to get children ready for the next stage of development. I remember vividly how my middle school social studies teacher insisted that we must do a complicated project so that we would be "ready" for high school. Why can't we accept a child where he is developmentally? Why do we always have to be thinking ahead and encouraging children to reach beyond their current capability to the next stage? This is a very inappropriate request.

Each and every human being should have the freedom to grow at his or her own rate, with the necessary support from the surrounding culture and society. Later in this chapter we will discuss ways to tackle this issue. We will introduce some ideas about education/learning methods and basic thoughts about reframing our relationships to each other. Below is a wonderful description about the importance of meeting a child where he is in his development. This posting is a dynamic and emotionally fueled statement about how humans feel about being cared for in a loving way.

Rachele Burke, http://womanuncensored.blogspot.com

Thursday, December 31, 2009

"Just let her cry"

1:06 AM

There was a time, not so long ago in my life, when I was nearly as helpless as a baby. It was a dark time in my life, when it should have been a radiant one. I was pregnant, and joyously happy about it, but my body was not. I was sick, and not in a "oh I don't feel so hot" kind of way. It was a "if I didn't have big things to live for, I'd want to die" kind of sick. Some of you may have experienced this too. I could literally not even hold down a sip of water or a nibble of food. Eating made me throw up. Not eating made me throw up. I would throw up stomach bile. Anyway, the point is that I was VERY weak. At 4 months pregnant, I weighed less than I did when I was 16 (and everyone called me stick girl back then). My clothes were falling off of me, instead of becoming tight. Every few days, I would be able to hold down maybe one meal's worth of food. In case you are wondering, it is called Hyperemesis Gravidarum, and it typically does not respond to medical or natural treatments. We tried anything that wouldn't be harmful to the baby, and nothing worked. Despite the physical misery, the emotional scars I suffered at the hands of a loved one were far more profound.

I grew so weak that I could rarely leave the bed. I needed support just walking the 10 feet to the bathroom. I needed a shower stool and help getting clean. Just raising my arms to wash my hair was an immense strain. I relied heavily on my husband.

My husband was loving during the day, but things would change at night. He would leave me in the bed, tell me it was time to sleep, shut off the lights, and walk out. I would say "But honey, I'm not ready to sleep yet" but he would ignore me. It was confusing. Sometimes, I'd be having a day where I felt I may be able to eat or drink something, and I would call out to him, asking for something. Again, he would ignore me. Sometimes he would poke his head in, but it was only to tell me that I needed to go to sleep and I was "fine". I had times where I grew very depressed. On top of being sick and miserable, I missed my husband's loving arms. Sometimes I just needed to be held and comforted. Still, he would ignore me. I began to wonder why my needs were valid during the day, but not at night. At times, he would leave the room far too cold or warm. Sometimes I desperately needed to use the bathroom. Sometimes the pain all over my body became unbearable. Sometimes I was just very scared and lonely. Alas, no matter what I felt or needed, my husband ignored me.

I longed desperately for my independence, and loathed needing another person for even the smallest things, but for the time being, there was nothing I could do but ask for enough help to at least keep myself and our baby alive. I was so hurt and confused. I would weep bitterly, alone in the dark. One night, I overheard my mother in law talking with my husband. She said "Just let her cry. She has to learn. Don't let her manipulate you, she doesn't really need anything. Keep it up and you'll win eventually." Win? What exactly was he going to win, and at what cost?

Eventually, I lost all trust in my husband. I would lie there in bed, hungry, hot, cold, hurting, and/or just plain sad and lonely. I stopped asking for help. I later heard my husband boast that he had finally "trained" me. So now I was an animal. Why did he get to decide what needs and feelings of mine were valid, and which were not? Why was it okay for him to be my husband during the day, to love me, talk with me, and help me, but at night time all my needs were expected to suddenly cease? I would never be able to fully trust or open my heart to him again.

In the darkest time of my life, my most beloved person failed to be there for me. My needs were small, things that would take very little time or effort, but were of great importance to my physical and emotional health. I was neglected. You may even call it abuse. Fortunately, it was a brief time in my life. Unfortunately, there are countless more victims of this kind of neglect, and even worse. They are even more helpless than I was. They are babies. Sweet, innocent babies. They have parents that love them fiercely and truly, but fall victim to beliefs and advice that (usually) inadvertently put babies on a level even lower than animals. Books and well-meaning friends or family tell tired new parents to "just let her cry". This is often referred to as CIO (cry-it-out) or "controlled crying", although the already twisted concept of controlled crying is often further misunderstood and warped and becomes "I let my baby scream for 2 hours and eventually she threw up and wasn't the same for weeks after".

Helpless babies are expected to cease all "neediness" once a certain time on the clock comes around. Their God/nature-given instincts to cry and express real physical AND emotional needs are ignored or written off as manipulation or just plain not "real" needs. Why? If a sick adult or an elderly person were treated in such a way, they would suffer in deep ways and the person responsible for their care could even end up in prison.

Why are babies treated as less than human? Why would we WANT to teach our children that we won't be there for them? Why should we get to pick and choose which needs are "real" and which ones are not? Why should our job as parents simply end at night? Just because they've been fed and changed doesn't mean they are "fine". All they have is their instincts. For all they know, a predator could be lurking and waiting to eat them! They are programmed by God/nature to want to be near us for their own safety and for their proper development. We know that human contact is essential to the developing brain of a baby, but we deny their natural pleas for such contact. We lock them in the dark and even though we may sing, pat them, and say "you're okay, sweetie", when we walk out of the room and leave them in the dark alone they may still be cold, hot, uncomfortable, in pain, or just plain scared or lonely! Why is that so wrong? "Cry it out" or "controlled crying" is just neglect with a different name.

Scientists everywhere know the short and long term consequences of these so-called "methods", and they are vast. Most parents also instinctually know these things. Some parents listen to those instincts, and others listen to people like my mother in law who say "Just let her cry. She has to learn. Don't let her manipulate you, she doesn't really need anything. Keep it up and you'll win eventually." These people usually mean well. They aren't setting out to harm a child, but that doesn't change the fact that they are. Argue with me all you want. Say "I let my baby cry it out, and he/she is fine". I don't believe you. I believe you broke your child like an animal. I believe they gave up. They didn't magically learn to "self-soothe", they just figured out that you suck at being a parent at night time. YOU will be old some day, or you may find yourself in a helpless situation even earlier than that. See how you feel if another person tells you what to feel, when to feel it, and how to express it. See how you feel if they ignore your feelings and only meet the needs that THEY deem valid. See how you feel if you are treated like less than an animal, someone that must be trained. Someone that must lose, so they can win. A baby has far less capacity to understand these things, so the next time your little helpless one cries out, remember that they cry for a reason. Even just wanting to be held is a real NEED. If you've ever seen what happens to those babies in foreign orphanages that never get held or talked to, you'll realize the incredible importance of human contact. It's so simple.

I could go on for days with even a million more reasons, but I will leave you with a few resources, and a simple piece of advice. Next time you hear "Just let him/her cry", think twice. You'll never regret being there for your child.

Women can have it all—just not all at the same time.

"Sequencing" is the concept coined by Arlene Rossen Cardoza (Cardoza, 1986) in her book by the same name. Cardoza describes a woman's different responsibilities as she moves through phases of her life. Mothering is one of the responsibilities that deserves her full attention. When she first enters adulthood, she may go to school to learn a trade or to get a general education, or she may find a job and begin earning a living. Along the way she may find a partner, become pregnant, and have a child. Now her responsibilities switch from focus on herself to being the primary care giver for that new life. The infant depends on his mother for everything and, initially, the mother is the only one who can meet the needs of her child. Very soon other family members will be able to become part of the child's network of support persons, but during the first three years of life the child genuinely needs to have his mother close by. That is the period when the mother-child attachment is developed. The bond created between the mother and child is critical for normal child development and a healthy adult life. All future interpersonal relationships are determined by the attachment a child has for his mother. Society has a responsibility to support this critical child development aspect.

[I believe} in motherhood as the nourishment of life...it is the most wonderful, satisfying thing we can do.

—Eunice Kennedy Shriver

Mother-Child Togetherness

We have a duty as a society to find creative ways for mothers and children to remain together during the early years of life. Child development theory has long recognized the importance of children being cared for by their primary caregiver (optimally, their mother) for the first three years of life. Child developmental theorists Jean Piaget, John Bowlby, Mary Ainsworth, Eric Erikson, and others clearly make the point that children who have a secure attachment to their mothers are able to maintain and establish appropriate relationships with others as they continue their development. They maintain that this full attachment takes about three years to develop. (Mooney, 2000) We need to address all the elements that make this such a challenging concept in the technological world of today. These include the financial realities of satisfying the economic situation of each family and societal pressures that often make women feel that they are not being productive members of society if they stay home with their young children in the early years.

We must address the workplace barriers for women to find those creative ways to remain the primary caregivers. Often women feel conflicted about going back to work after the birth of a baby. Either real or perceived societal pressures affect women in their thinking about returning to the workplace. They feel that if they give up their jobs to stay home with their children they will never be able to reenter their fields at the same place that they left. They feel that society won't respect them for their decision to stay at home.

Concern about the safety of the child care environment in both physical and emotional dimensions can be an important issue. The cost of child care can make the whole thought of returning to work seem almost impossible. Many women spend several days' income out of each week just paying for child care. If we add to that number the cost of a work wardrobe, and the cost of prepared food because of the convenience and time issues experienced by the mother, it is a wonder that women have any wages left to put in the bank. Maybe we need to refocus our attention on finding creative ways for mothers and children to stay together in the early years. In the future we can commit ourselves to looking for opportunities for women to make a living while remaining with their children.

Real Life Example

My father recently went to live in an assisted living environment where the employees are encouraged to bring their children to work with them. In this way, everyone benefits. Instead of separating our elderly citizens from being in the presence of young people, this community has found a way to integrate them into the community. It is mutually beneficial for all parties. The employer has happy employees, the children have their mothers or fathers nearby, and the residents enjoy the interaction with young people. The residents can focus on the good in life rather than their ailments and disabilities. In addition, the children have the experience of older, wiser people in their lives with lots of time and wonderful stories to share.

Mother-Child Separation

In days gone by, families often lived in the same geographical area as much of their extended family. Common practice was that a family member would care for young children if their moms needed to go to work. In this way, children were cared for by people with whom they had been familiar since birth and who loved them as if they were their own.

Today we have a much different situation. Family make-up has changed. Many families are having trouble making ends meet, and finding ways to support the family while preserving the integrity of the mother-child attachment has become an ever-present dilemma.

What does this do to the attachment between mother and child? As a society we have ignored this question far too long. Since the women's movement of the 1960's and 1970's we have lived in a society with many questions about the roles of women. Maybe now is the time to take a look at how women's roles have changed and what values we can pinpoint as important as we move forward to redefine how women live in the 21st century. The following excerpt from *What Our Mothers Didn't Tell Us* by Danielle Crittenden gives us a clearer picture of how the feminist movement of the 1960's and 1970's is affecting us in the world of today:

> ***The urgent and compelling questions that haunt us from moment to moment are ones to which the women's movement offers no answers—or when it does, answers that are unhelpful. Is work really more important and fulfilling than raising my children? Why does my boyfriend not want to get married as much as I do? Why is the balance between being a good mother and working so elusive? Why could my mother afford to stay home with her children while I cannot? By giving up my job, am I giving up my identity? Should men and women be trying to lead identical kinds of lives, or were there good reasons for the old divisions of labor between mother and father, husband and wife? If so, do these divisions make us "unequal"?***
>
> —*What Our Mothers Didn't Tell Us,* Danielle Crittenden

Now it is time to ask: What about the mother-child bond? What consequences will our society face—is already facing—as the result of broken attachments in our children?

Do we support an environment that acknowledges a child's right and need to be with his mother for the first three years of life? Or do we advocate for a societal environment where mothering of the young child is not seen as important enough to find a way for mothers to stay home until their children reach at least three years of age?

Healthy brain development depends on a young child's attachment to his mother in the critical first three years of life. Depriving a child of his mother's presence for long periods of time many days each week can have long reaching effects on the child's ability to develop in a normal manner. (Mooney, Theories of Attachment, 2010) This fact cannot be taken lightly. We must assure that mothers are able to stay in close contact with their young children during most of their waking hours. Because children develop at varying rates as they grow beyond infancy, the need for mother's constant presence in the child's world becomes less important. By the time a child reaches the age of three, most will have developed the maturity to be separated from the mom for short periods of time.

All families need to advocate for the well-being of their children. Our society needs to encourage parents to be aware and alert to the needs of their children. We must have the ability to find creative ways to meet the needs of our children, thus allowing them the freedom to develop into well-adjusted, secure human beings.

Using creative and innovative programming, we might begin to explore shared work schedules with mothers watching one another's children while they work. Bringing young children to work might be an option in many more places than we see it today. In many instances young children can be integrated into the work environment. Our society has the opportunity to think outside the box and to open our eyes to the possibilities. Certainly a babe in arms can be worn in a wrap and just come along with the mom to work in many situations. For example, childbirth educators, teachers of many kinds, a variety of office workers may all be able to complete their work with their young babies in tow. As children grow into toddlerhood, many situations still can allow for children to be present with some supervision. Allowing women to take some time out during their work day to stay in close contact with their young children when needed would certainly make huge differences in the attachment process. It would not only be good for the children but would also allow the mothers to feel more satisfied with the work that they are able to complete, knowing that their children are not being compromised in the process.

When all work options have been explored and the mother determines that she must leave her child with a caregiver she must consider all the elements of the child care setting before she can embark on the search for an optimal situation.

Here are some things that need to be in place to protect the fragile mother-baby bond:

- Encourage mothers to stay home as long as possible after the birth of their baby.
- Search for creative alternatives to mother-baby separation (i.e., work from home, work reduced hours, work alternative hours).
- Minimize the amount of time young children need to be separated from their mothers.
- Make sure that mothers and babies can continue their important intimate relationship throughout the day by providing space in the work environment for them to remain together as much as possible.
- Create more opportunities for job sharing.
- Allow mothers to work flexible hours.

There are other examples of mother-child separation caused by societal constructs inappropriate to normal mother-child attachment. These include hospital policies that require parents to separate from their children during medical procedures or parents not being allowed to spend the night with a hospitalized child. This separation often results in unnecessary stress for both mother and child. Attached children do better when the mother-child relationship is left intact. When we have policies that allow mothers and children to remain together at these difficult times in a family's life, we can work together as a team to care for the whole child in the way most appropriate for his development and well-being.

Learning Environments/Education

Educating versus Learning

Take a few moments to read the following quotations and to think about our cultural ideas on education and learning.

No one asks how to motivate a baby. A baby naturally explores everything it can get at, unless restraining forces have already been at work. And this tendency doesn't die out, it's wiped out.

—B.F. Skinner, *Walden Two*, original copyright 1948)

I noticed a dangerously detrimental misapprehension about the nature of intelligence. For many educators and students, it appeared that intelligence was not only measured by, but equated with knowledge. I believe this to be an entirely false assumption, because knowledge is only the by-product of a curious mind. It is not how much we know but, rather, how much we want to know that determines the brightness of our minds. I believe that curiosity is intelligence in its purest form….

—Valya Boutenko, *How We Came to Eat Raw Food*, pages 8 and 9, 2008

When I left Connecticut it wasn't with the ambition of peddling. I had yearned to be a teacher. It seemed to

me that most schools went about the work of instruction backward, crushing children's natural curiosity and deafening them to the wisdom of their own internal voice.

—Geraldine Brooks, *March*, 2005

What are your thoughts about the ideas presented in the above quotations? Your impressions will color the way you look at the discussion that follows. Each of us has a historical context to bring to the discussion. We may be motivated by the kind of educational settings that we have experienced in our own life, or we may be influenced by the kinds of places that we envision as being better or worse than what we experienced. All of this depends on how we feel about the way we have received information in the past.

To lay a framework for our discussion it is necessary for us all to be on the same page as far as the definitions we are using for the words "education" and "learning." For our purpose let's define education as the system by which people receive information. In other words, education is the formal model with which we go about personal learning. It is based primarily on a top-down model of decision makers planning what information should be taught to learners. Learning, on the other hand, is individual-centered, meaning that the person wanting to receive information is at the center of the process. The learner is the one in control of what he wants to learn and how he wants to learn it. For the purpose of this discussion we must keep this distinction in mind.

Our society is always pushing children to get them ready for the next stage. Why? Can't we just let children be who they are today? Do we have to push them to the next stage of development? Child Development theory would tell us that we are wasting our time trying to get children ready for what comes next. Children will learn what they are ready to learn, when they are ready to learn it. No amount of pushing and prodding will help children move through their personal development faster.

Let's not push them beyond their capability. Let's let them just "be" who they are. Child development is a sequential process. We discussed this briefly earlier in this section. Piaget's child development strategy is the basis for how we must look at what happens to children during their learning process. The process will take place as it should all by itself. We don't have to worry about it, or try to push it.

In addition to Piaget's ideas of child development, we need to also look at developmental psychologist L.S, Vygotsky's ideas on the Zone of Proximal Development (ZPD). This zone is the area that exists between a child's developmental ability to complete a task on his own and to complete it with the help of others.

Vygotsky would say that a child's ability to acquire a full range of skills in a particular field of study depends heavily on the child's ability to interact socially, because many children need the additional information provided by others to achieve their maximum potential in a particular subject area. His social development theory is in response to the readiness for learning that we see in children when they hit definite developmental milestones.

A child's curiosity must be nurtured and supported. When we recognize this inquisitiveness as of the utmost importance, we must be moved to offer the very best opportunities to our children in terms of learning choices.

The Learning Process: How Does It Work?

Play is a child's work. We must never forget that a child learns through his experiences with the world around him. He uses his imagination to practice communication styles and relationship building. When children "play house" they have opportunities to be the mother, the father, the brother, the sister, the grandma, and so on. This helps them build an understanding about the world by seeing situations from other points of view. The child may find out a lot about himself. He may find the kinds of activities that resonate with him. Does he enjoy being a leader? Does he like working with his hands? Does he like getting messy? Does he enjoy activities where he can be outside? The list of possibilities goes on and on. Yet, in our current educational system a child rarely has a chance to have these kinds of experiences that enrich lives.

When you think back to your early memories about school, what positive experiences do you remember most? Most likely you remember the field trips you took to the zoo or the bakery, or the walk to the fire station or the police department. You might remember the play you were in while in high school or the concert where you played the violin. Our fondest memories of school usually are experiences rooted in our right-brain memory. When we remember the feelings associated with the event, we can recall many of the details and can describe the situation as if it happened yesterday. These memories have been imprinted because we were highly involved in the experience.

Today we have a name for this kind of learning. We call it experiential education. The term often refers to informal educational opportunities like summer camp, often intense sessions of several weeks where children live in a kind of "alternative universe." They are immersed in the experience, living it day and night. The real world seems to dissolve away and the child dives into his experience with both feet. Can we make this kind of experiential learning the norm rather than the exception? I believe we can.

We must seriously discuss our school system and the way children learn. As a credentialed teacher, I have had over three decades of experience working and being involved in the public school system in the United States. I have had the opportunity to participate in the system as a student, a teacher, and a parent. What I have come away with, after all this time, is the knowledge that the United States educational system is not meeting the needs of many children.

There are a few basic reasons for this. The present U.S. educational system was designed to be a top-down model. We set up a system based on teachers and principals deciding what children needed to learn, and then we set out programs to meet those identified requirements. Instead of implementing programs that could meet the individual needs of each student, the programs were designed to meet the needs of the "average" student.

It turns out that there is really no such thing as the average student. Each child is a unique individual with a unique set of needs. Yes, learners can sometimes be grouped at specific points in their learning experiences when a particular skill or concept is needed by a group of students at the same time. However, this is not likely to happen with a group of thirty students in the third grade at the same time. Our present system was set up so that one teacher could teach a group of 25 to 35 students at one time. This system no longer works. The information age has changed everything about how children can access information. Our educational system, however, is still trying, in large part, to use the old model of having children sit at their desks for many hours every day. Typically children study subjects in isolation (one subject at a time, unrelated to another). On the other hand, integrating curriculum (relating several subject areas in one project) would allow children to find ways to experience material in a more "real world" view. (See section on Learning Styles for more about this.)

Teachers have long been semi-independent to arrange their classrooms as they see fit to address the perceived needs of the students in their care. However, today teachers have an almost impossible task. With 30-35 students in a single classroom and one adult responsible for the education of those children, one can understand how overwhelmed and ineffective the classroom teacher can be.

Under the present system it is nearly impossible to clearly identify each student's needs on a daily, weekly, or even monthly basis and to group and regroup the students according to their progress and ever-changing needs.

The system was set up to accommodate the capabilities of this educational model. Today, of course, on top of the regular curriculum teachers have been required to meet additional criteria to prove that they and their schools are meeting baseline standards of the school district and county, state, and federal governing agencies that support education. The result of this accountability has been the death knell for the school system as we have known it. Children are suffering in a myriad of ways. They are stressed about homework, plagued by test taking, and left questioning many concepts that the teacher doesn't have time to fully explain because of the oversight of the governing agencies. Teachers spend so much of their time fulfilling their responsibilities to their employers that it is a miracle the students are getting any time at all to have their curiosity satisfied. Teaching now requires so much recordkeeping and administration that the wonderful vocation of sharing the joy of learning with students has all but disappeared.

Many wonderful teachers are leaving the teaching field for less stressful, more satisfying work that lines their pockets with more dollars. Teaching has become a career fraught with all kinds of problems, including behavioral problems from the students. Could this be a manifestation of students who are bored, challenged beyond their capabilities, or overburdened with societal responsibilities and situations (i.e., caring for siblings while parents work, teen pregnancy, and working to help support the family)?

Many high school teachers I have spoken to in the past several years talk about schooling as a babysitting situation—a place to keep the students off the streets. Learning is not the primary task in the minds of these teachers. Although the mission of the school system is to educate the learners, the reality of the situation is often not coming close to the desired outcome.

Our system was put in place at the beginning of our nation when we saw students as little adults who needed to be told what to do and how to do it. Children are not mini-adults. They have very specific needs at each stage of their development that must be met. We cannot rush this process.

Most young people come to school at the age of five knowing so much more than the Baby Boomers when they entered kindergarten. The average kindergarten curriculum today looks much like the first grade of fifty years ago. Children haven't changed developmentally, and yet our curriculum has accelerated their expected skill acquisition by a whole year. This is a problem.

Children's ability is not taken into account when curriculum changes are made. Instead of looking at how to change the curriculum to better educate our children, we need to look at what is appropriate for children at any given developmental stage and design curriculum to meet their capabilities.

What can we do about this? Redesigning the learning environment to be bottom up, instead of top down would go a long way in starting to address the current problems with the school system. This means that we would take a close look at the learners. In fact, we would involve the learners in decision-making regarding what the curriculum should look like and what they are interested in learning about. Instead of looking at children as students, we might begin to think of each of us—young and old—as lifelong learners. The difference in language is an important beginning. A student is a more passive role. Teachers deliver education to the students. A learner is someone who has taken an active role in his or her learning/education. Learners seek information and resources. They need help from those around them to facilitate finding the information that they are interested in learning.

If we began to make changes to the public educational models that we currently use by reframing the way we look at the system, we will begin to see learners actively engaged in the process. When we ask children what they are interested in learning and listen to what they say, we will find a renewed excitement and energy in the educational process.

To get to this place, much must be accomplished. However, it is something that can and must be done if we are to have a viable learning environment for the generations of today and tomorrow. The ways of the past are no longer working. We must find new, innovative ways to engage the learners of today. The good news is all we have to do is ask the children and listen to what they tell us. If we build networks of adults, both within the educational system and from outside, who are excited about the possibilities of offering our young people a learning environment that will be interesting and stimulating for all involved, then progress can be made quickly.

There are wonderful books available that will guide interested people in this most noble pursuit. Start with books about democratic education like the list of titles from the Sudbury Valley schools. (See Reference List.)

What sets these kinds of programs apart from the traditional school setting? This is an easy question to answer. The system we have in place today is broken. When education is dictated from the top by people who are not involved on a day-to-day basis with children we often find rules put in place that require teachers to be accountable to the system by quantitative measures. Test scores, written reports, and particular curricular requirements may be put in place to measure performance. However, is that measuring how well the children are actually doing in the program? Usually not.

It is the qualitative elements that really matters, but they cannot be as easily measured. Much more time and subjective measurement techniques are required to evaluate the quality of a program. The children are the losers in the current situation.

We must look to the children (the learners!) for the answers to how to develop a learning environment that can be successful in today's world. Instead of seeing teachers as the ones who should be making the decisions about when and what children are going to "learn," we can find out from the children what they would like to learn. Democratic education models are a great place to start. John Holt's books about progressive education are as true today as they were when he wrote them. (Holt, 1995)

Actively involving children in the design process for curriculum can be an invaluable method for ensuring a successful learning program. When the student is included in the process, the result is much more likely to be relevant and accepted by the student.

Learning Styles

The concept of learning styles is one that we need to visit at this juncture. All people have a primary learning style. These styles include auditory-, visual-, and tactile-related elements. Most of us are aware that we relate to information in a variety of ways, and we are often clear on what kinds of information or style of learning is predominant for us. However, classical education models frequently ignore or don't take our learning styles seriously. This is another place where our educational system sometimes fails. When teachers are aware of the learning styles of their students, they are much better able to offer learning opportunities that will allow those students to achieve mastery of the information being taught.

Learning Environments

Learning environments that use an integrated-curriculum approach or a unit-of-study approach often allow learners to work on projects that will allow many learning styles to have the opportunity to shine. For example, a unit of study on birds might include reading books about birds and making an oral presentation about what one learned. That would be a project in which a linguistically talented child would excel. The body-smart child who needs to move around to internalize information might need to take a hike to see the birds out in their natural environment and then come back to his learning setting to build a bird house or make a bird feeder using materials that he collected on the hike. A musically talented child might find a website on the internet to listen to the sounds that different birds make and then write a piece of music that reminds her of the sounds that she heard. These are just a few examples of how a multi-disciplinary approach can meet the needs of a variety of learning styles. (For More on this subject see my article footnoted below.)

Exploring ways to improve our educational system will open many doors for our children. In our role as advocates for our children

---

Deutsch Lash, Margie, *Multiple Intelligences and the Search for Creative Teaching,* **Paths of Learning, Issue 22, Autumn 2004, pp. 13-15.**

we must discuss and implement the necessary changes in our learning institutions that will enable our young people to meet the intense demands of the technological society in which we live. Our children's future depends on our leadership to find the answers.

We can't solve problems by using the same kind of thinking we used when we created them.

—Albert Einstein

Change Must Come

We must embrace change as we search for ways in which we can address the dilemmas we have identified. Many times when people are aware of major societal problems, they feel overwhelmed and wish to close their eyes and hope that someone else will tackle the hard questions and the even harder actions that must take place to move society to this better place. In this section you will be offered a list of the possible changes that address the majority of the issues raised in previous chapters.

As we embark on the path for change, let's open our minds to the possibilities. The potential is limitless when we put our minds to work to establish our priorities. As we make a plan that will enhance our society, we will make way for a future that is full of promise.

Action Items:

<u>Join an advocacy organization that works on issues important to women and children – for example:</u>

www.momsrising.org

www.LLLI.org

www.oxfam.org

www.oxfamamerica.org

www.waba.org.my/

Lobby your employer for a flexible work schedule for mothers of very young children. Sharing information about the benefits of this kind of creative arrangement will not only educate employers but also will empower parents to put their energy into working on projects.

Develop networks of women who will support each other. Examples of these kinds of formal or informal groups are internet-based groups like attachment parenting groups (www.attachmentparenting.org) or La Leche League (local groups available in many communities throughout the world, www.llli.org).

Think about creative solutions and alternatives for women returning to work (i.e., working from home, bringing the baby to work, looking for new opportunities that will bring in income that would allow mom to stay home).

Be involved in implementing and support policies that allow parents to remain with their child during hospital procedures and hospitalizations. Keeping parents and children together at key times during a child's life are of paramount importance. When children are frightened and vulnerable they need their parents more than at any other time.

Spend quality time with your children whenever possible. Rather than providing diversions with MP3 players, hand-held video games, and DVD players, why not take this valuable time to actually interact with your child? *Really* communicate. Don't be afraid or overwhelmed. Try it; you'll like it.

Use every opportunity to stay connected. Next time you are in a car, on the bus, or traveling on the subway, talk to your child about his hopes and dreams and about your own. Plane travel can be a wonderful opportunity for a family to have that much-needed time to interact on a level often difficult to come by. One has concentrated time to really communicate their hopes and dreams—their very values—to their children when presented with an opportunity of long travel. Long car travel presents the same kind of opportunity.

Set values that clearly support your family.

Clearly articulate your values to your children.

Limit or eliminate time spent using electronic equipment, watching television, or Playing video/computer games

Create an environment for you and the children in your life that includes doing something for others. The act of giving broadens your horizons and that of your children. When we show compassion and caring for others, we extend ourselves. The benefits we gain from this kind of sharing of ourselves come back many times over.

Volunteer your time. Opportunities for sharing are available through community organizations, religious institutions, and all kinds of non-profit agencies. Reach out to others.

Support your favorite charity financially. This kind of giving becomes a shared value by our children when they are aware that their parents and the other adults in their life share their resources with others. Encourage your children to choose the charity of their choice.

Have dinner together as a family most nights. Set a regular time whenever possible. Communicate about your plans for the day before the day begins so that ever family member is clear about the plans for dinner each night. Set appropriate expectations. In other words, focus on being together. Dinner time is a part of the day to share. Often parents use this time to get compliance by setting lots of rules that sometimes foster an adversarial relationship between family members. Instead foster cooperation and mutual respect. This can be done by working together as a family to get dinner on the table. Each family member can have a responsibility for something—setting the table, washing the vegetables, mixing the ingredients together. Even young children can help. Remove distractions like television during meal time. Encourage each family member to talk about their day.

Encourage reading by reading to your children and being a reader yourself.

Expose the children in your life to cultural activities in the arts—music, drama, visual arts—by spending time together at concerts, plays, and museum exhibitions. All kinds of free and inexpensive opportunities are available throughout communities around the globe. Just seek them out.

Reach outside your own experience by taking part in activities that push you outside your comfort zone. This will be great modeling for your children, too.

Interact with people of varying cultures. Don't allow the differences between us as human beings of diverse cultures, races, nationalities, and religions to get in the way of our human relationships and interconnectedness. Go to an exhibit of African art, a display of Chinese ceremonial objects, a traditional East Indian dance performance, or participate in a musical celebration in a style different from your own cultural background.

Make time in your day just to be present with your children. Over-programming can be a major downfall for the family.

Work with local, state, and federal officials to support legislation that addresses things like:

Family Leave

Workplace initiatives

Health care

Education

Let's Work Together

With today's global community, we have the unique opportunity to effect change in a big way. As a result of our ability to communicate with people all over the world in a matter of minutes, we should be able to start making changes quickly. It is a matter of communicating the ideas. Learning these concepts is not dependent on economic or governmental support. All we need to do is start to educate people about why it is so important to keep mothers and babies together.

Let's begin now. Take your list of ideas, develop them in greater detail. Talk to those around you—in your community, at work, people you sit next to on the bus or train. Let's make this process come alive. Let's begin to work on getting our world to a place where children will have all that they need from society to develop into well-adjusted, healthy citizens both physically and mentally.

REFERENCE LIST

(23 September 2010) Why Cavemen were better parents than we are today. *Daily Mail*. Retrieved from www.dailymail.co.uk/news/article-1314452/Why-cavemen-better-parents-today.html

Academy of Breastfeeding Medicine (ABM). (2003). *Guideline on co-sleeping and breastfeeding* [Online content]. Retrieved from http://www.bfmed.org/protocol/cosleeping.pdf

Bergman, N. J., Linley, L. L., & Fawcus, S. R. (2004). Randomized controlled trial of skin-to-skin contact from birth versus conventional incubator for physiological stabilization in 1200- to 2199-gram newborns. *Acta Paediatr, 93*, 779–785. doi: 10.1080/08035250410028534

Black, J., Kagle, J., & Haight, W. (2003). Understanding and supporting parent-child relationships during foster care visit: Attachment theory and research. *Social Work, 48 (2)*, 195–207. doi: 3299823821.

Bowlby, J., Attachment and Loss, (1980) Volumes I – III New York, Basic Books

Bowlby, J. (1996). *A Secure Base Parent-child Attachment and Healthy Human Development*. London: Routledge.

Caplan, M. (1998). *Untouched: The Need for Genuine Affection in an Impersonal World*. Prescott, AZ: Hohm Press.

Cardoza, A. R. (1986). *Sequencing*. New York: Atheneum.

Cassidy, J., & Mohr, J. (2001). Unsolvable fear, trauma, and psychopathology: Theory, research, and clinical considerations related to disorganized attachment across the life span. *Clinical Psychology: Science and Practice, 8(3)*, 275–298.

Coleman, P., & Watson, A. (2000). Infant attachment as a dynamic system. *Human Development, 43 (6)*, 295–313.

Colson, S. D., Meek, J. H., & Hawdon, J. M. (2008). Optimal positions for the release of primitive neonatal reflexes stimulating breastfeeding. *Early Human Development, 84*, 441–449. doi: 10.1016/j.earlhumdev.2007.12.003

Duhn, L. (2010). The importance of touch in the development of attachment. *Advances in Neonatal Care, 10(6)*, 294–300. doi: 10.1097/ANC.0b013e3181fd2263

Falceto, O. G., Giugliani, E. R., & Fernandes C. L. (2004). Influence of parental mental health on early termination of breast-feeding: A case-control study. *Journal of the American Board of Family Practice, 17(3)*, 173–183.

Fergerson, S. S., Jamieson, D. J., & Lindsay, M. (2002). Diagnosing postpartum depression: Can we do better? *American Journal of Obstetrics & Gynecology, 186(5)*, 899-902.

Fox, S. I. (1993). *Human Physiology* (4th ed., pp. 176-178, 264) Dubuque, IA: William C. Brown Publishers.

Geddes Productions. (Producer). (1992). *Dr. Lennart Righard's Delivery Self-Attachment* [DVD]. Available from http://www.geddesproduction.com/breast-feeding-delivery-selfattachment.php

Gerhardt, S. (2004). *Why Love Matters: How Affection Shapes a Baby's Brain*. New York Brunner-Routledge.

Greenberg, D. (1991) *Free at Last: The Sudbury Valley School.* Framingham, MA: Sudbury Valley School.

Greenberg, D. (1992). E*ducation in America: a View from Sudbury Valley*. Framingham, MA: Sudbury Valley School.

Greenberg, D., Greenberg, H., Greenberg, M., Ransom, L., & White, A. (1992). *The Sudbury Valley School Experience*. Framingham, MA: Sudbury Valley School.

Greenberg, D., & Sadofsky, M. (1992). *Legacy of Trust: Life after the Sudbury Valley School Experience*. Framingham, MA: Sudbury Valley School.

Greenberg, D., & Sadofsky, M. (1998). *Starting a Sudbury School: A Summary of the Experiences of Fifteen Start-up Groups*. Framingham, MA: Sudbury Valley School.

Harlow, H. F., & Harlow, M. K. (1966). Learning to love. *American Scientist, 54(3),* 244–272.

Henderson, J.J., Evans, S.F., Straton, J.A., Priest, S.R., & Hagan R. (2003). Impact of postnatal depression on breastfeeding duration. *Birth, 30(3),* 175–180. "Early cessation of breastfeeding was…significantly associated with postnatal depression…Onset of PND occurred before cessation of breastfeeding in most cases."

Hofer, M.A. (1995). Hidden regulators: Implications for a new understanding of attachment, separation and loss. In S. Goldberg, R. Muir, & J. Kerr (Eds.) *Attachment Theory: Social, Developmental and Clinical Perspectives* (pp. 203–230). Hillsdale, NJ: The Analytic Press.

Holt, J. (1995). *How Children Learn*. Redding, MA: Addison-Wesley.

Hunter, B. (1997). *The Power of Mother Love*. Colorado Springs, CO: Waterbrook Press.

Karen, R. (1994) *Becoming Attached.* New York: Warner Books, Inc.

Karr-Morse, R. & Wiley, M. (1997) *Ghosts from the Nursery*. New York: Atlantic Monthly Press.

Kendall-Tackett, K. (2004). *Lactation Consultant Series 2, Unit 8. Postpartum Depression and the Breastfeeding Mother*. Schaumburg, IL: La Leche League International.

Kertzer, D. I., Sigle, W., & White, M. J., (1999). Childhood mortality and quality of care among abandoned children in nineteenth-century Italy. *Population Studies, 53(3),* 303-315.

Kinsley, C. H. & Lambert, K. G. (2006) The maternal brain. *Scientific American*.

Klaus, M. (1998). Mother and infant: Early emotional ties. *Pediatrics, 102,* 1244-6. doi: 10.1542/peds.102.5SEI.1244

Klaus, M. H., Kennell, J. H., & Klaus, P.H. (1995) *Bonding: Building the Foundations of Secure Attachment and Independence*. New York: Addison-Wesley Publishing Co.

Kroeger, M. (with Smith, L. J.) (2004). *Impact of Birthing Practices on Breastfeeding: Protecting the Mother and Baby Continuum*. Sudbury, MA: Jones and Bartlett.

La Leche League International. (2003). *The Breastfeeding Answer Book* (3rd ed.), Schaumberg, IL: Author.

Lauwers, J., & Swisher, A. (2005). *Counseling the Nursing Mother* (4th ed.) Sudbury, MA: Jones and Bartlett.

Lawrence, R. A. (2005). *Breastfeeding: A Guide for the Medical Profession*. Philadelphia: Mosby-Yearbook, Inc.

Lewis, T., Amini, Fari, & Lannon, Richard. (2000) *A General Theory of Love*. New York: Random House.Liedloff, J. (1975) *The Continuum*

Concept: Allowing Human Nature to Work Successfully. Reading, MA: Addison-Wesley.

Lyons, H. (2007). Attachment theory and reactive attachment disorder: Theoretical perspectives and treatment implications. *Journal of Child and Adolescent Psychiatric Nursing, 20 (1)*, 27–29.

Maki, P. *Parental separation at birth and maternal depressed mood in pregnancy: Associations with schizophrenia and criminality in the offspring* (Unpublished doctorial dissertation). University of Oulu, Oulu, Finland.

McCain, M. N., & Mustard, J. F. (1999). *Reversing the Real Brain Drain: Early years study final report*. Ontario: Ontario Children's Secretarial.

McGoldrick, M. (1994). The ache for home. Family Networker, 18(4), 38-45.

Menacker, F. (2005). Trends in Cesarean Rates for First Births and Repeat Cesarean Rates for Low-Risk Women: United States 1990–2003. *National Vital Statistics Reports, 54(4)*, 1–8.

Minkkinen, M. H., *Infant Brain development and the impact of breast feeding: A review of literature* (Unpublished doctorial dissertation). University of Minnesota Duluth, Duluth, MN.

Mogi, K., Nagsawa, M., & Kikusui, T. (2010). Developmental consequences and biological significance of mother-infant bonding. *Progress in Neuropsycholpharmacology Biological Psychiatry, 35*, 1232–1241.

Mooney, C. G. (2000). *Theories of Childhood: an Introduction to Dewey, Montessori, Erikson, Piaget and Vygotsky*. St. Paul, MN: Redleaf.

Mooney, C. G. (2010). *Theories of Attachment*. St. Paul, MN: Redleaf.

National Commission for Culture and the Arts. (2008). *Social Life in the New Stone Age* [Online content]. Retrieved from http://www.ncca.gov.ph/about-culture-and-arts/e-books/e-book.php?id=10&t=1.

Newman, J. & Kernerman, E. (2009) *The importance of skin to skin contact* [Online content]. Retrieved from:http://www.nbci.ca/index.php?option=com–content&view=article&id=...

Nielsen, M. P., Olausson, P. O., & Ingemarsson, I. M. (2007). The Cesarean Section Rate in Sweden: The end of the rise. *Birth, 21(1),* 34–38.

Noel-Weiss, J., Woodend, A.K., Peterson, W.E., Gibb, W. & Groll, D.L. (2011) An observational study of associations among maternal fluids during parturition, neonatal output, and breastfed newborn weight loss. *International Breastfeeding Journal, 6,* 9. doi: 10.1186/1746-4358-6-9

Odent, M. (2001). *The Scientification of Love*. London: Free Association Books.

Odent, M. (2003). *Birth and Breastfeeding*. East Sussex: Clairview Books.

Olanders, M. (2004). *Early skin-to-skin contact for mothers and their healthy newborn infants (RHL commentary).* Retrieved from The WHO Reproductive Health Library website: http://apps.who.int/rhl/newborn/gpcom/en/index.html

Parenting the Stone Age Way, StraitsTimes Indonesia, Jakarta Globe, (2011)

Righard, L., & Alade, M.O. (1990). Effect of delivery room routines on success of first breast-feed. *Lancet, 336,* 1105–1107.

Riordan, J. (2005). *Breastfeeding and Human Lactation* (3rd ed.), Sudbury: Jones and Bartlett.

Ryan, J. (2009) Is postpartum due to not breastfeeding? *Contemporary Pediatrics*

Schore, Allan N. (1994), Affect Regulation and the Origin of the Self: The Neurobiology of Emotional Development, Hillsdale, New Jersey, Lawrence Erblaum Associates.

Schore, Allan N. (2003), Affect Regulation and Disorders of the Self, New York, W.W. Norton & Company.

Schore, A.N. (2001). Effects of a secure attachment relationship on right brain development, affect regulation, and infant mental health. *Infant Mental Health Journal, 22(1-2),* 7–66.

Schore, A. N. (2002) Dysregulation of the right brain: a fundamental mechanism of traumatic attachment and the psychopathogenesis of posttraumatic stress disorder. *Australian and New Zealand Journal of Psychiatry, 36,* 9–30.

Sepkoski, C. M., Lester, B. M., Ostheimer, G. W., & Brazelton, T. B. (1992). The Effects of Maternal Epidural Anesthesia on Neonatal Behavior during the First Month. *Developmental Medicine and Child Neurology, 34,* 1072–1080. doi: 10.1111/j.1469-8749.1992.tb11419.x

Small, M. (1998). *Our Babies, Ourselves: How Biology and Culture Shape the Way We Parent.* New York: Anchor Books.

Small, M. F. (2002) What you can learn from drunk monkeys. *Discover,* 23 (7), 40-47.

Smith, L. J., (2010). *Impact of Birthing Practices on Breastfeeding* (2nd ed.). Sudbury, MA: Jones and Bartlett.

Sørensen, H. J., Mortensen, E. L., Reinisch, J. M., & Mednick, S. A. (2006) Early weaning and hospitalization with alcohol-related diagnoses in adult life. *American Journal of Psychiatry, 163*, 704–709. doi: 10.1176/appi.ajp.163.4.704

Star Foundation. (2001). *The Psychology of Birth.* [VHS]. Geyserville, CA: Producer.

Taj, R., & Sikander K. S. (2003). Effects of maternal depression on breastfeeding. *Journal of the Pakistan Medical Association, 53(1),* 8–11.

Taveras, Elsie M., Capra, Angela M., Braveman, Paula A., Jensvold, Nancy G., Escobar, Gabiel J., Lieu, Tracy A.,(2003). Clinician support and psychosocial risk factors associated with breastfeeding discontinuation. *Pediatrics, 112(1),* 108–115.

Thoman, E. B. (1975). Early development of sleeping behavior in infants. In N. R. Ellis (Ed.) *Aberrant Development in Infancy.* New York: John Wiley.

U.S. Department of Health and Human Services, Office of the Surgeon General. (2011). *The Surgeon General's Call to Action to Support Breastfeeding.* Washington, DC: Government Printing Office. Retrieved from http://www.surgeongeneral.gov/topics/breastfeeding/calltoactiontosupportbreastfeeding.pdf

Van Sleuwen, B. E., Engelberts, A.C., Boere-Boonekamp, M. M., Kuis, W., Schulpen, T. W. J., & L'Hoir, M. P. (2007). Swaddling: A systematic review. *Pediatrics, 120,* e1097–e1106. doi: 10.1542/peds.2006-2083

Walker, M. (1992). Summary of the Hazards of Infant Formula, International Lactation Consultant Association

Walker, M. (1998). "Summary of the Hazards of Infant Formula, Part 2", International Lactation Consultant Association

Walker, M. (2004). "Summary of the Hazards of Infant Formula, Monograph 3", International Lactation Consultant Association, 2004

Wagner, M. (2005). Midwifery and International Maternity Care. *Midwifery Today, 75,* 12–13.

Weed, S. S., (1986). *Wise Woman Herbal for the Childbearing Year.* New York: Ash Tree Publishing.

Wiessinger, D., West, D., & Pitman, T. (2010). *The Womanly Art of Breastfeeding.* New York: Ballantine Books.

What Would Mammals Do? http://conciouswoman.org/2007/01/06?what-would-mammals-do/

Williams, N. (1997). Maternal psychological issues in the experience of breastfeeding. *Journal of Human Lactation*, 13(1), 57-60.

Printed in Great Britain
by Amazon.co.uk, Ltd.,
Marston Gate.